TEACHING VOICE

Workshops for Young Performers

Max Hafler

NICK HERN BOOKS
London
www.nickhernbooks.co.uk

A Nick Hern Book

Teaching Voice: Workshops for Young Performers
first published in Great Britain in 2016
by Nick Hern Books Limited,
The Glasshouse, 49a Goldhawk Road, London W12 8QP

Cover images © Shutterstock.com/g-stockstudio

Designed and typeset by Nick Hern Books
Printed and bound in Great Britain by Ashford Colour Press,
Gosport, Hampshire

A CIP catalogue record for this book is available
from the British Library

ISBN 978 1 84842 579 8

Contents

'If you are teaching, you must be active.
You must not give the impression of activity.
You must be active…
Try to speak as if from your whole being.'

Michael Chekhov,
Lessons for Teachers

Preface

This book is for those youth theatre leaders, schoolteachers or lecturers teaching non-vocational theatre courses or programmes who want to help their students to develop their voices, either as a component in theatre training, for a short time when they embark on a play, or for the benefit of their everyday lives.

If you have done some voice work, either on short courses, or through speech and drama, and are open to new exercises and new ways of teaching, this book is for you. It should give you some ideas to help with vocal challenges, and innovative exercises mixed in with the tried and true.

Whilst this book is *not* a substitute for a training course – to me, experiential learning is always the best way to learn this process – it sets out some pathways to give you the confidence and basic tools to begin working on voice with your young people.

Voice work is vital for well-being. It improves relaxation, communication and self-confidence. It is helpful in job interviews, presentations, or if the young person is entering a profession in which she has to talk a lot and convey ideas and feelings. So it is a vital part of the wider educative ethos to give your students 'a voice'.

It is not only for acting.

How to Use This Book

I am well aware that there will be many readers who need structured support in order to make ideas meaningful for the young people they are teaching, so I have tried to provide that by creating a course of nine sessions, followed by a series of micro sessions, and concluding with two sessions for more advanced work.

However, because seven of the sessions are very much *themed*, there is nothing to stop the more experienced of you cherry-picking sessions and basic work.

It all depends on your own level of experience, the type of group you are working with and the circumstances under which you are working.

First Steps

The Introduction explores why it is so important to help our young people work on their voices, and the crucial part that voice, and especially breathing, plays in their health, development, and ability to express themselves.

It also includes an exercise programme for *you*. Depending on your skill level and interest I hope you might find this useful, to develop your own skills and confidence around the subject. Teaching voice requires an experiential knowledge which is found through your own observation, your own practice and your own body.

The Two Core Sessions

Part 1 features two full plans for ninety-minute core sessions: basic voice introduction sessions where you will lay the foundations for the other work. Roughly speaking, they explore breath, diction, resonance and relaxation. They include some fun exercises as well as the basic floor work. Schoolteachers or those with less time available may need to split each session into two. These sessions focus initially on practical, exercise-based work and then move towards the more imaginative approach.

What works for your group depends very much on what kind of group they are, how many there are, their ages, and where you are working with them. These sessions are fundamental to the other work.

The Seven Themed Sessions

Part 2 sets out seven themed workshop plans of roughly seventy-five minutes' duration, each on a particular aspect of voice work: projection, rhythm, the power of language, voice in realistic drama, emphasis, working with experimental sound work, and exploring Shakespeare. You might find any or all of these useful, particularly in terms of the kind of work your youth theatre, school group or college might be intending to tackle.

The Micro Sessions

Appreciating that time is sometimes of the essence, Part 3 contains a series of micro sessions which serve the same kind of purpose as a short session in a yoga book. They keep your group alive to the importance of voice and give them an exercise or two to explore. Micro sessions assert the value of voice within the structure of any session, however restricted your time frame might be. They may be good for the less experienced teacher/facilitator also, as a place to start.

The Further Sessions

Part 4 concerns incorporating voice work in rehearsal for production in either a school or youth theatre setting, and then on developing the work further.

And finally, the appendices feature a bibliography, a list of organisations and individuals you might be interested in contacting, and a basic voice warm-up sheet you might want to use as a template – and which is also available as a downloadable resource on the Nick Hern Books website: www.nickhernbooks.co.uk/teachingvoice

I hope you find this book useful and fun, and that it may lead to more young people opening, exploring and developing the power of their voices.

Please note: In respect of the fact that people will use different entry points for this book, I established this rule: I have not repeated the full instructions for exercises which I describe in full in the early workshops, then recur later, as it would have made the book rather long. So I will refer you back to when the exercise first appears. The only time I have broken that rule is with the micro sessions, where there is a basic explanation, in case you decide to go there early on to get your group familiar with voice work.

Thanks

To Matt Applewhite and all at Nick Hern Books, and to Benet Catty.

To Rebecca Bartlett and Niamh Dillon in particular for their encouragement and support of my work at Galway Youth Theatre and the Blue Teapots.

To all at the National Association of Youth Drama, Ireland, for giving me the opportunity to explore working with voice with generations of young people all over Ireland. Thanks especially to Dave Kelly, Ella Daly, the members of Dublin Youth Theatre who appear in the photographs and Sean T. O'Meallaigh for taking them.

To the participants: Leah Minto (facilitator), Debbie Murphy (facilitator), Aine O'Hara, Marcus Vaughan, Conor Kelly, Lee Stafford, Evan Sunderland, Niamh Elliott-Sheridan, Caroline Flood, Austin Sheedy, Sean Talbot, Sean Guthrie.

To Paddy Swanson, Janna Lindstrom, Debra Salem, Ulli Meyer-Horsch, Sarah Kane and Bruce Myers for showing me some exercises that I have developed or used in this book. To Ted Pugh, Joanna Merlin, Fern Sloan, Lenard Petit and the other extraordinary teachers of the Michael Chekhov Association.

To Florence Robinson, who taught me voice and acting long before I went to drama school; to Joyce Morris for her encouragement and support; to my family, and to my partner

Tony Hegarty who has taught me a phenomenal amount, especially about teaching. Thank you, Tony, also, for the many suggestions, and the proofing of the initial manuscript.

To Robert Klottrup for his great voice teaching when I was at drama school.

And, last but not least, to all the groups both young and older with whom I have worked, and who have gone on the journey of exploring voice.

Max Hafler

The author and publisher gratefully acknowledge permission to quote from the following: 'Tarantella' from *Sonnets and Verse* by Hilaire Belloc, reprinted by permission of Peters Fraser & Dunlop (www.petersfraserdunlop.com) on behalf of the Estate of Hilaire Belloc. *The Caucasian Chalk Circle* by Bertolt Brecht, translated by James and Tania Stern with W. H. Auden © Bloomsbury Methuen Drama, an imprint of Bloomsbury Publishing Plc. 'The Listeners' in *The Golden Treasury* by Walter de la Mare, reproduced by permission of the Literary Trustees of Walter de la Mare and The Society of Authors as their representative. *Murder in the Cathedral* by T.S. Eliot, published and reproduced by permission of Faber and Faber Ltd. *Blood Wedding* by Federico García Lorca, translated by Jo Clifford, published and reproduced by permission of Nick Hern Books Ltd. *Under Milk Wood* by Dylan Thomas, copyright © 1952 by Dylan Thomas. Published by Phoenix, and reproduced by permission of the Trustees for the Copyrights of Dylan Thomas. Every effort has been made to trace copyright holders, but if any have been inadvertently overlooked, the publisher will be pleased to make the necessary arrangements at the first opportunity.

Introduction
Why Do Voice?

'The voice is the most intricate mixture of what you
hear, how you hear it and how you unconsciously
choose to use it.'

Cicely Berry

This introduction outlines the challenges and reasons for teaching voice, and offers support and suggestions to the facilitator/ teacher. There is also some discussion of the Michael Chekhov Technique and the connection of voice, imagination and body. In addition to explaining the mechanics of breath, the chapter also offers a short preparation session for the facilitator to touch base and enable them to go more slowly and deeply.

Setting the Scene

If there's a temptation to skip on to the workshops, tips and exercises which make up the main part of this book, I would suggest you don't surrender to it, because this Introduction is going to help you engage with the exercises and workshops within a certain context, and I would suggest it may make the workshop plans even more useful.

When we consider all the other important things we could be doing with our groups in the thin window of time in which we see them each week, what makes voice so important?

1

I am a strong believer in having an ethos for any training. It gives our facilitating and teaching focus and strength. I would like to talk here about some of my own influences, and why I think they are important, so you will understand my ethos and viewpoint. I would also like to discuss some basic breathing theory so I do not need to spend too much time on it during the core session plans.

Finally in this Introduction, I suggest a short programme for you to start with on your own, exercises using a somewhat slower, more internal approach for your *own* development so that you can be more confident when you teach.

The Wider Issues

There are broad challenges to exploring voice work, especially for young people.

The idea that sounds and voices can take you anywhere and are keys to the opening of worlds is evaporating. With abbreviation and the spoon-feeding of our imaginations with someone else's commercial ready-made images in films, TV and on the internet, words and language seem to be less and less important. We need to awaken or remind young people of the power and beauty of the spoken voice; what you can do with it; how it empowers you; how it is an instrument of your personality, your feelings and your very essence. The voice work we do with our young people has to have this as its aim.

But change can be challenging. Cicely Berry, the iconic voice teacher, revolutionised voice training by asking us to consider the social and psychological pressures on us all to speak and breathe a certain way. She wrote, decades ago in her seminal book *Voice and the Actor*: 'Because it is such a personal statement, criticism of your voice is very close to criticism of yourself, and can often be seen as destructive.'

So we have to be very sensitive in our approach.

A crucial aspect of voice training is relaxation, or I would prefer to use Michael Chekhov's expression, which is to inhabit a *feeling of ease.* Initially we are going to put a lot of focus on breathing.

We should consider the power of the diaphragmatic breath, which is scientifically proven to promote relaxation. It is a useful tool for young people, who are frequently tense and stressed – and should be taught to them, whether they are going to act or not. Learning about this breathing from the diaphragm may also stimulate them to practise at home, even if they do not imagine they will ever act professionally. Being aware and in control of the breath makes a person feel more confident.

The voice that is well articulated, relaxed and connected to the body, imagination and feelings is vital for well-being. Voice work improves our capacity to communicate. Let us consider for a moment the pantheon of jobs that require a clear and expressive voice: teacher, lecturer, lawyer, solicitor, shop assistant, care worker, youth leader, phone worker, canvasser, bus driver, ticket collector, tour guide, politician, anyone who works for the public service (and on and on)... and that's before we get to actors.

When it comes to acting, though, you *are* your instrument. When you go on stage you are playing upon your body, voice, imagination and feelings. Everything. No young person can do adequate justice to how they feel, or their ideas (especially in some of the acoustically challenging venues in which youth theatres and schools find themselves playing) without some voice work.

Voice ought to be considered as part of the wide social and educational remit of youth theatre, schools or any liberal-arts course. By doing voice work, you are literally giving the young person a 'voice'.

Practical Challenges

The Clock

Most youth theatres meet for two to three hours per week. In that time you have to warm up, rehearse or devise, have fun, and involve yourself in some kind of pastoral caring exchange when required. Schools and many college courses do not have much time either. Of course, the occasional workshop can be fun and will hopefully give your young people a feeling of release. Crucially though, the basis of much early voice work involves a lot of practice and repetition. How can we inspire them with the idea that voice is important to them and get them to practise when we are squeezing the voice work in?

I would suggest that after one or more full voice sessions you might like to run 'micro sessions': short periods within your workshop which consciously concentrate wholly and fully upon voice. This is why I have, after the programme of themed sessions, created a number of micro sessions, on roughly the same topics. It will mean you will be able to mix, match and adapt to your own and the group's needs.

It might also be important for you to provide basic workout sheets for support and encouragement, should the group want to practise and pursue the work in their own time.

Age

Voice work can be practised by any age group, you just need to adapt the work. The exercises in this book are primarily for groups aged between fourteen and twenty, but many of the exercises can be used for a younger group with adaptation, time adjustment, or by changing the teaching goal. I use many of the same exercises with adults but with a slightly different focus or vocabulary. More on this later.

Focus

Voice might not be the main focus of your group at this time. We need to balance the issue of meeting the participants *where they are*, with the skills and opportunities that the setting (be it youth theatre, school or college) allows them. Offered at the wrong moment, too much voice work might frighten them off. I don't want to overemphasise this fear, because young people can also be very nervous about using their bodies in anything other than the most inhibited fashion. In other words, the young person's inhibition is not just a voice issue.

By including some structured voice work, you are in fact freeing the young person to express herself more effectively. Of course, the timing for your group has to be right for it to be really beneficial. Only you can know when that is.

Within the school setting this fear of being judged and therefore remaining inhibited is incredibly strong, and in this environment I would suggest you move very slowly indeed. Floor work might be challenging in this context, for instance, but I will provide guidance on this later.

Different Settings

Anyone who has run the same youth theatre for some time has had the experience of the organically changing needs of the group. A fluctuation in the needs of the group is something we need to consider in our decision to teach voice. It needs to be the right time.

Youth theatres seem to fall into four distinct types. These types can be fluid, as different facilitators and participants come and go and projects and interests develop.

The Shows-and-Skills Youth Theatre

This is the youth theatre that puts on regular plays and is looking for traditional theatre skills to support them. They may do scripted plays or devised work. They tend to be more production-based, rather than process-based. The participants are usually pretty motivated, and often a number of them have their sights set on an artistic career. The process and production ought to be of equal importance, because whenever we do plays or drama, issues inevitably develop for the young people.

The Devised-Work Youth Theatre

This type of youth theatre is very much focused on process, exploring the views of its young people and helping make those views into theatre. They tend to be less focused on traditional skills, but focus more on making work that expresses their ideas and feelings. They frequently get round their lack of traditional skills by presenting powerful work in smaller non-theatre venues. They are totally engaged with the creation of the work. Finding both their collective voice and the individual voices within them is paramount.

The Social-Space Youth Theatre

The primary aim of this group is to give support in a myriad of ways to young people and give them a worthwhile activity. Their agendas for being there are usually social and the drama is very much a sideline activity, even though they might enjoy it. Here the *process* is the primary aspect of the interaction. A production, however, can often focus the group in a way nothing else could.

Schools or Colleges

These groups present quite a different set of opportunities and challenges to the above. In school, you are wrestling with the requirements of the curriculum, the issues in the institution, the way the young people feel about school, the fact that some people will be very hard to win over, the peer pressure (which, whilst it can be strong in the other sorts of group, is even more acute in schools). Some of the more expansive exercises might be challenging, so you need to tread cautiously. You are asking people to be brave and a saboteur can be extremely destructive. Depending on your group, I might suggest sticking to technical elements, relaxation and games initially, until you have the group ready to go into other areas.

Speaking 'Proper'

Voice work for youth theatre does not equate in any way with the 'speech and drama' approach or, even worse, elocution. There are some similar goals because we want people to achieve clarity, but these elements need to be taught and experienced completely differently. Our work needs to be enjoyable and liberating, and as imaginative as it is disciplined. Whilst voice work can seem tedious and repetitive, it is essential we find ways to make it interesting and dynamic, and relate it not only to acting but to the demands of the participants' everyday lives. Much of the way this can happen is by using the body, imagination and movement to explore the voice fully. It can be fun.

At no time should we be trying to eradicate the natural accent of a young person, nor is it in our remit to deal with a speech 'impediment'. The goal must be for the participant to find an open voice that is clear, relaxed, confident and expressive. If they practise, of course, their voices might well change, and nothing delights me more than when a young person whose voice is whispered and weak discovers she can make a rich loud sound.

When working on Shakespeare scenes or full productions with young people in Ireland, I have many times been asked, 'Should we speak in an English accent?' This goes to show that the feeling that one does not speak 'properly' is alive and well, and that there is some kind of *proper* way to speak. I always assure them that what I want them to do is connect with the words, characters, story, sensations, feelings and ideas, and that their breathing, bodies and imaginations need to connect to the language in order that they might share all that with their fellow actors and the audience, rather than worry about their accents.

If you as a facilitator have some ambivalent feelings towards the idea of teaching voice, you need to start considering them. Perhaps you are concerned with how your group might receive this kind of work. Certain groups I have worked with would not have thanked you for anything you might have even loosely called voice exercises. I remember one particular group in working-class Dublin whose work was incredibly authentic and involved powerful site-specific work set in their own community. I felt I managed to convince them by explaining that they were a group with ideas, valuable ideas which they wanted to share through theatre, but that without some vocal skills they were not going to be able to promote their ideas effectively. These ideas could also be explored through their voices, and we did a whole weekend on writing, rap, soundscapes and speaking chorus. But we also did a lot of regular voice work which introduced them to clarity, breath and relaxation.

Owning and Adapting Exercises

Recently a teacher told me that while she personally got a lot out of doing a facilitators' weekend workshop with me, she felt afraid or uncomfortable using the material we had worked on with her own group. This fear can partly be a nervousness around the whole subject of voice, or can be an idea that exercises you learn elsewhere do not somehow belong to you. Let that idea go.

In addition to my own original exercises, I use many which were taught to me as a student, or I have learned them from fellow professionals and adapted them as I've gone along. The exercises become yours the more you use them. This is perfectly natural. Own them and change them. Many of my own original exercises are now used by ex-students of mine.

Once, whilst working at MIT in Boston, I was asked to do some outreach work with an LGBT youth theatre group. I was doing warm-up exercises with them. One of the voice and movement exercises began, and their facilitator who was there to help me, suddenly cried out, '*That* is one of Paddy Swanson's exercises!' I was amazed to hear him use the name of someone who had taught me decades before, and whom I had not seen since the seventies. I did not think for a moment that this was not my exercise because I had developed and refined it for years. It was totally my own: I actually met Paddy later and told him what a great influence he had had on my work. It was a lovely opportunity to thank him.

Adapting exercises can be an extraordinary journey. Good exercises are multilayered and have many different aims. You need to decide what the main focus of the exercise might be for your group – this may not be the focus for which it was intended. When we adapt an exercise, we need to decide what we feel it teaches or opens for the young person, and then do what we need to do to make it work *for the group*. This aspect of inclusion is absolutely crucial. For example, once when I was running my pre-professional course in Voice, I wanted to use a particular breathing exercise, which started out with each student kneeling on the ground. It was based on a yoga exercise and was quite strenuous. I had a very committed and amazing young woman in the group who had a disability and used a walking frame, so I adapted the exercise to have the students seated astride chairs. The movement involved a similar spinal movement and a feeling of a core of breath beginning from the very centre of being and rising to the ceiling. It worked for the whole class. Now I use it often with chairs because it is easier for all less supple people and is much more relaxing.

Michael Chekhov Technique

Though he was not a voice teacher per se, Michael Chekhov has had the most impact upon me, both in terms of my voice work and my directing and teaching in other fields, principally because of his faith in the *body* and the *imagination* to plumb the creativity of the human being.

Michael Chekhov (1891–1955) was one of the most innovative actor/director/teachers of the twentieth century. A nephew of the great playwright Anton Chekhov, he acted in the Moscow Art Theatre with extraordinary success, occasionally coming into conflict with the director Stanislavsky and others that worked there. His journey across Europe and eventually to the United States – where he acted in Hollywood movies (most notably in Hitchcock's *Spellbound*) and taught and influenced a whole number of famous and less famous actors – is one of both frustration and triumph. His belief in the creative imagination and use of the body to find sensations and feelings for the character makes acting into a truly magical art of extraordinary potential. Whilst he was not a voice teacher, he was very interested in the work of Rudolf Steiner (1861–1925) whose creation 'Eurythmy' involved a whole physical language to correspond to sound.

Michael Chekhov Technique makes the connection between voice, imagination, body and feelings. Why is this so very important? It makes us into whole people and whole performers. It gives us an *awareness*, and opens doors. This should be one of our prime aims when working with young people, if it is at all possible. Our body should be our friend, and it can be, if we loosen it up and make it porous to all the sensitive influences of which it is capable. Young people tend to have very polarised views about their bodies, from freedom and elasticity, to tense, uneasy and closed. This can be a challenge for them and for us, but using the body to free breath, feelings and language is healthy and positive. Along with the body, the other actor's friend is the imagination.

The Power of the Imagination

Whilst facilitating a voice and relaxation course for the Blue Teapots Theatre Company in Galway, Ireland, a training and performance programme for young adults with learning difficulties, I discovered that in order to get the participants to exercise meaningfully and with energy, I needed to use images rather than instructions to stimulate them into using their voices and bodies in expressive ways. For instance, instead of saying, 'Exercise your fingers,' I might say, 'Pretend you are playing the piano.' When I used this approach they were much more free.

Previously with youth theatre or drama students I had primarily used energy and playfulness to encourage an intellectual and muscular understanding of the body, the voice and breathing. It involved a lot of physicality, but not so much imagination. With the Teapots it was the imagination that was key and it began a big shift in my approach.

Words and images react within you when you read a novel and you create your own world prompted by them. It is a charged reaction. When you see the movie of the same novel it is frequently disappointing because the images presented are not *your* images. The film is simply not the way you imagined it. What's worse is that those movie images can never change, whereas when you re-read a book the images can change.

A useful Chekhov exercise is to imagine a character in a fairy story in every detail, then consciously imagine it differently. Your own images can help you speak with more feeling and power.

Exploring through imagination sometimes involves a risk, especially for teenagers who often consider themselves above such childlike processes and for whom taking that risk might expose them to looking or feeling foolish. Working imaginatively can remind some young people of primary school, and they might feel they are beyond it. Work with the imagination demands they let go of this fear. Reminding them that acting has its roots in 'Let's Pretend' can often be reassuring. Still, for some, working primarily from the imagination is not intellectual or 'adult' enough for them and smacks of an esoteric, 'hippy-dippy' exploration. We can observe this fear of using instinct/imagination regularly in workshops when groups are under pressure to produce a piece of work and then spend the whole of their preparation time discussing the possibilities rather than getting up and exploring them.

If they dare to imagine and try, the results can be easier to achieve and more groundbreaking than purely muscular and intellectual practice and understanding.

However, voice is *movement* so there are a lot of plusses to drills and routines. Some people respond well to them, and because much voice work is involved with technical prowess, drills are essential and need to be made fun. Some young people love set warm-ups; they give that feeling of ensemble, focus and togetherness which is one of the massive wider learning arcs of engaging young people in theatre. They are always a mainstay of my own work. But they are not everything.

I have learned to vary the exercises, some using the physical energy trigger, and some which use imagination as the key. Try to keep this balance and you will not only be helping the participant to understand the mechanics of voice, but to explore imaginatively and powerfully their inner potential. For example, you can ask your group to put their voices in their chests, or you can ask them to imagine they are filled with brown and make a 'brown' sound. Both approaches are important, the mechanical and the imaginative.

Breathing: The Key to Everything

It may be that you are a youth theatre worker or teacher who has done *some* training, but much of your voice training has been made up of an occasional workshop here and there. You have done some practical theatre and maybe some speech and drama. Maybe you have done some singing training. What you have *not* done most likely is a consistent professional voice training. Whilst this book is *not* a substitute for that training, it can help to give you the confidence to teach some basic voice, and then develop and make your own discoveries.

Relaxation classes or yoga are excellent for breathing, and any voice classes or courses you might be able to attend are useful. However, singing classes may be less helpful because, although so much of their training involves listening, diction and breathing, there are some fundamental differences.

The reason for this is that many singing teachers focus on rib breathing *first*. This is not a good plan with tense young people, who, when they try to breathe into their ribs, will inevitably breathe into their chests and shoulders, tightening their whole upper bodies. You have a very short time with your group so you have to do what you can to find the door that will lead quickly to that open, liberating breath.

INTRODUCTION

Some Theory

Breath is the absolute bedrock of teaching voice. Teachers often talk about breath *control.* Whilst we might be trying to achieve control, control immediately implies tension, which is the last thing you need to explore with this work. Rather than control, I prefer to say *freedom*, or *power.*

Breath is the fuel for everything we do; body movements and functions, even thoughts, and speech. Without breath we are dead. So the more easily and fully we can breathe, the better we can function and most certainly the better we can act and speak. As I mentioned earlier, it has been scientifically proven that diaphragmatic breathing triggers the relaxation response. We frequently notice this change in our own breathing especially after a stressful day when our breathing might be high in our chests. Just as we are falling asleep we feel the breathing deepen and fall into the belly.

So what is this 'belly-breathing'? We are not literally breathing into the belly, of course, but the movement of the diaphragm downwards makes it feel that way.

The diaphragm is a large muscle attached to the ribs and the spinal column. When we breathe in, the diaphragm muscle extends downwards allowing air to come into the lungs. This makes the tummy move outwards as the organs are pushed downwards. Many teenagers are reluctant to allow this because they fear it will make them look fat, but once they understand the vocal power such breathing gives them and that it makes them feel relaxed, they frequently feel easier about it.

When you breathe out and you push the stomach muscles *gently* in, the tummy flattens as the diaphragm muscle relaxes up to its original position. Try always to get participants to breathe in through the nose and out through the mouth, as that is what you do when talking. Over the page are two photographs of the facilitator firstly breathing in, with the tummy extended, and then having fully breathed out, with the tummy slightly pulled in.

13

Breathing in

Breathing out

You need to reassure your group that it is natural for the ribs to move, but they should not be the focus for the breath. The ribs should not feel like they are the destination for the intake of breath. It is as if the breath passes the ribs and ends up in the belly.

We will explore later in more detail how you can tell whether someone is *breathing down*, how you observe this and then how to help the young person dissolve any tension that might be making this process uneasy. You will need to consider how they breathe, and who takes shallow breaths and who doesn't, if you are going to help them.

Let's forget about the young people for a minute and begin with your *own* practice. Here is a warm-up specifically tailored to you. You can incorporate exercises from the workshop plans as you get more proficient, but for a few weeks, for your own practice, stick with this.

I have restricted this little practice to about fifteen to twenty minutes maximum. Take it slowly. Do it in the morning three or four times a week, or every morning if you can manage it. It is a space for you to familiarise and calm yourself with a few basics in the work. There is no point in telling yourself the young people should explore voice if you are not prepared to explore it too.

Also, knowing this breathing work *intellectually* is not the same as putting it into your body. The exercises for you in this section are deep and you should take your time with them.

I want you to try and work holistically, both with yourself and with your group, in order that everyone gets the most out of it. Much of the voice work we will do is very physical, not only because that quickly loosens up the participants and is more fun, but also because what we are seeking is a link between voice, breath, body and imagination, so they become a dynamic whole.

This is not only good for acting, but for life.

Find a room that is warm and comfortable and where you will not be disturbed, with enough room to lie on the floor.

Your Own Warm-up

Breathe Down

- Stand with your legs shoulder-width apart, feet parallel and knees slightly bent, arms hanging by the sides. Notice when you bend the knees it relaxes the lower back. Do not push the pelvis forward, just let it fall a little.

- Imagine you are holding a beach ball between your knees so that they do not collapse in too much. Feel the feet on the floor and imagine your feet are reaching into the earth, getting their nourishment from the earth like the roots of a tree. When I say 'imagine', what I mean is *invite that image into you*. Don't struggle, just invite the image in. Let it be there.

- Now, look ahead. Imagine you are breathing down into the earth. Notice if your shoulders rise and/or your chest expands. If this is happening, re-imagine the idea of breathing down, and see if you can sink the breath lower into your body. Get a sense of the breath going down to your groin almost. Do not force it, though. Keep the whole thing easy. It will happen eventually. If you try too hard you will only create tension.

- Now, still breathing gently, raise both arms up as if you are holding the large beach ball between your chest, arms and fingers (see below). Make sure the thumbs are easy and if they are not, then bring your attention to them and tell them to 'let go'. This *standing position* is a *Qigong* exercise, an Eastern form of exercise related to t'ai chi. (More information about this practice can be found in *The Way of Energy* by Master Lam Kam Chuen, Gaia Books.)

- As you let go of tension and find comfort in the position, feel the energy stream round your body; any tension, focus on it, and tell it to let go. Keep that focus and stillness going for two to three minutes.

- Breathe in and very gently, *with* the breath, open up the arms. See if you can feel a connection between the breath and the movement of the arms. When the arms are wide, try not to over-extend them behind you, just keep your hands a little forward of the body.

- Then breathe out and bring your arms back in to the beach-ball position. Do this four times.

- Bring your arms to your sides. Then, as you breathe in, slowly raise them as if you are transcribing an arc with your fingers, over your head; as if you are drawing a rainbow over your head. Your hands are palms up.

- In the space between the in- and out-breaths, turn your hands so that the palms are down. Breathe out and bring your arms in the same arc back to your sides. Repeat four times. Breathing in through the nose, out through the mouth. Try not to overstretch your elbows.

The purpose of this exercise is for you to connect the body with the breath and therefore the voice. It both calms and focuses.

Massage and Melt

- Gently massage your scalp and face, paying particular attention to the hinge of the jaw. Draw your hands down the face slowly. If it helps you, try imagining the hinge of the jaw melting a little, and the space between the eyebrows melting a little. Massage the neck too. Imagine it is wet clay or a pot you are moulding.

- Then rotate your shoulders forward very slowly, and incorporate the whole body almost like you were skiing in slow motion. Then take the shoulders back in a circle the other way.

This exercise is important to develop a feeling of ease and dissolve tension in the upper body.

Basic Floor Exercise

- Lie down, slowly and easily, flat on the floor and feel your breathing. Do not criticise or judge the way you breathe. Feel where your body is in touch with the floor. If your neck or head is uncomfortable you may need to put a book under your head to align your spine more comfortably. Let all the stress or concerns of the day seep out through the floor, or on an out-breath sigh. Do that for a few times until you feel completely in the here and now, breathing on the floor.

- Raise your knees and put your feet flat on the floor. Feel your body in contact with the floor. Breathe in and gently curl the pelvis off the floor, just as much as is comfortable. Hold it there for a moment, and then breathe out and allow the pelvis back down smoothly. Repeat this a few times.

- Lying in the same position, lift the shoulders from the floor then let them fall. Repeat a few times. Then, turn the head gently from side to side. Repeat a few times. Bring it back to the centre.

- Now focus on the face. Imagine the jaw hinge melting and the spot between the eyebrows softening.

- Place your hands on your tummy, remembering this is your belt line, and *not* your ribs. Start to imagine the breath streaming in through the nose, down into the lungs and *as if* it is moving under your hands. You might like to think of it gathering there as a soft bowl of air. Now very, very gently pull the stomach in and let the air out of your mouth. Allow just the sound of the air to come from your lips. Imagine that the air has been on this journey from the atmosphere then deep into your lungs, and imaginatively at least, down into your belly. It has actually passed through the whole body, oxygenating the blood. Spend a few minutes with this, breathing in and out.

- Put the fingers of one hand about two inches in front of your mouth, shape your lips into a soft 'O'. Breathe in through the nose, let the belly fill out, push the stomach in gently, which makes you breathe out and feel the breath passing the lips and hitting the fingers.

- You might like to try voicing a sound gently. If you feel any tension as the breath makes its journey, feel where it is. Bring your attention to that place, feel the tension and then tell the tense place, just 'let go'. It is important to use sound first rather than text, as even the most innocent sentence might send the body running back to its regular way of breathing and the tensions that go with it.

- When you have completed these floor exercises, roll onto your side, stay in that position for a few seconds and then get up *slowly*. The system can sometimes be overwhelmed by the amount of oxygen and you need to take your time getting up.

You will find further developments of this crucial part of the work in the group sessions and can incorporate them into your own practice.

This is a vital sequence in connecting the belly with the breath and the sound. A slightly different version forms a core exercise of the basic session for your group. If you are saying, 'Oh, I know this already,' it still might be useful to touch base and do some practice.

Finding and Radiating the Ideal Centre

I would like to do a little work on the Ideal Centre as described by Michael Chekhov. I will describe the exercise and then focus a little on why it is so important for voice (even though it isn't actually a voice exercise).

- Stand with your knees slightly bent, feet firmly on the floor. Close your eyes. Feel the energy of the earth beneath your feet, as if your legs are reaching into the earth, like the roots of a tree.

- Imagine the energy of the earth beneath your feet as golden, benign and moving, full of potential, full of power. Then start to feel that same energy in your whole body; warm energy coming up through the soles of your feet and moving through the whole body. Feel that it is energy not only in your body but also emanating from it. Stay with that feeling for a moment.

- Then imagine the sun is in your chest, strong and moving. Imagine that is the centre from which all your impulses come. Movements. Thoughts. Feelings. The impulse to speak. Try not to force this. Let any intellectual hindrances go. Focus on the idea that this warm heart centre is there for you, easily, and totally accessible.

- Focus on your middle fingers, and take your mind on a journey from there to your warm chest centre, through palms, wrists, forearms, elbows, upper arm, shoulder then across your chest, to the centre. Then focus on the ends of your big toes and take your mind on a journey up through your foot, ankle, calf, knee, thigh, pelvis, belly and spine, up to your golden centre.

- Try, with your eyes closed, to move your arms from that centre, and open them wide, breathe out as you open. When your arms are wide, try opening your eyes, and imagine the warm centre is filling the whole room. Bring your arms down and see if you can retain that imagination/sensation. Try saying a line from a text. See how that feels. Do not worry at this stage if you do not have enough breath to fulfil a strong sound.

Finding your Ideal Centre is an incredibly valuable exercise for actors and non-actors alike, and challenges our idea of projection. Projection is not just about breath and clarity; it is about radiating energies, and words and thoughts. If you radiate your energy strongly you do not have to over-project your voice. This exercise takes practice, but is well worth the effort.

Working Your Tongue and Lips

- Swallow and yawn first before you start this little exercise. Notice how this relaxes the throat and the back of the mouth.

- Chew imaginary gum both vigorously (x5) and then really slowly (x5). Keep alternating. Notice how you are much more conscious of the movement when you go slowly.

- Now make a circle with the tongue, inside the mouth around the outside of the teeth, very slowly, in a clockwise direction (x4), then anticlockwise (x4). Repeat moving your tongue around the inside of your teeth. Keep the lips closed.

- Try to touch your nose with the tip of your tongue, then your chin. Do that a few times and then stick out your tongue and move it from side to side.

- Make the tongue into a straw, by sticking your tongue out, then drawing up the sides of the tongue if you can, and then roll your '*rrrs*' if you can do it.

- Very slowly and quietly make a '*tuh*' sound. Take note of where the sound is being made – the tip of the tongue at the back of the teeth.

- Try a '*buh*' – make it soft, a plosive on the lips, then stronger and more defined.

- '*Kuh*' – feel the movement at the back of the mouth.

- '*Duh*' – the tip of the tongue higher than '*tuh*' on the palate.

- '*Suh.*'

- '*Fuh.*'

- '*Puh.*'

Exercising the muscles of your lips, face and tongue is vital to give words and consonants their full value. There are plenty of dexterity exercises later on. These slow exercises are to bring your attention towards how you make the consonantal sounds. For some people this awareness is a very new experience.

The Hum

- Stand in the *Qigong* position (page 16), with your feet parallel, knees bent, back straight, arms raised as if you are holding a large beach ball to your chest. Breathe in and down for a moment as you did earlier.

- On an *out*-breath, bring up one arm and put your hand on the crown of your head, and bring the other to your belly. Try and breathe down into the belly. As you breathe, imagine the breath like a river and a small boat is riding the current in, then coming back out of your mouth.

- Now close your mouth and breathe in to your belly. As you breathe out, hum with closed mouth. Try and focus your attention under the hand on your head. See if the hand tingles.

- When you have breathed out fully, bring your fingers to the bridge of your nose as you breathe in. Now hum out again, and try and place the resonance in the bridge of your nose.

- Breathe in and move your hand to touch the lips. Breathe out and focus the breath on the lips. Hum there.

- Breathe in and move your hand to your chest. Breathe out and make the chest vibrate on a hum.

- Finally and gently try moving the hum freely from one place to another. Notice how the voice changes. Breathe when you need to.

Working with resonance is crucial for variety, ease, emotional colour and projection.

Ready to Go

- Just massage your neck and shoulders a little, and then stand in the *Qigong* position with your knees bent, your back straight and feet parallel.

- Stand still and notice how differently you feel for doing this little bit of exercise. I guarantee you will feel more relaxed, more ready to work, more in the present.

- Imagine a line on the ground in front of you. Try and get a sense of the Ideal Centre from the earlier exercise. Feel where you are and know that when you cross that line, *cross the threshold* (another Chekhov term), you are walking into your session with a strong desire to teach.

- Notice how that feels for a moment then take a step back over the line and notice how you feel now.

- Then decide to step over the threshold again.

This powerful exercise works as well for imagining your entrance onto a stage as it does for the facilitator's entrance into a hall or studio.

Exercise in the Everyday

This is not so much an exercise but an outlook. A way to learn.

As you go about your day just notice how you breathe in everyday life. Notice where the breath is centred for you, in other words, where there is most energy, most movement. What do you sense is the destination of the breath as you breathe in? Is it in the belly, the ribs, or the chest? Do your shoulders rise as you breathe in? If they do, but only occasionally, notice when those times are. Do you feel you breathe differently when you speak?

Be conscious.

Standing in a queue at the supermarket, or finding yourself alone for two minutes, use the *Breathe Down* exercise (page 15). You will notice a calming effect. The more you get into the habit of this, the more it will work for you. Notice that when you speak, if the diaphragmatic breath is not integrated, tension comes into another area of your body as you speak and your breathing changes. Maybe it becomes shallower. It might take a little while for that integration of diaphragmatic breathing and speaking to happen. Don't worry. For now just notice it.

If you have to go to the shops, for example, see how it is if you try to find your Ideal Centre. See if you can maintain it as you speak to people, and go about your daily life. Get a sense of what that feels like.

Notice when tension builds in the body during the daytime. Tell the tense area to relax.

What you are trying to create here is an opportunity to become aware of your own body in a positive way. Then you can better help the participants in your groups to do it too.

In order for you to be able to help your group, you need to be thinking and engaging with the voice work through observation, not just of yourself but also of others. Play detective. Look at other people and try and guess how they are breathing. See if you can detect if there is any tension when they speak. Try and imagine where that might be. Notice if their breath is shallow. Are they always gasping, running to the end of their breath so the voice tightens or dwindles off? What impression does that give you of how they might be feeling? Do they speak too quickly? Do their voices exist in a monotone, or are their patterns and rhythms fluid and varied? See if you can chart this amongst your family members or workmates when you are not teaching.

To teach voice well in this workshop environment, you need to diagnose basic issues quickly. Sometimes it will be very obvious why a young person is having problems, sometimes not. *Please note*: I am not encouraging you to diagnose until you are ready to do so, which may be some time away depending on your level of experience – but these observation exercises can speed up the process considerably and help you a lot with your own practice.

You can add or take away from this warm-up programme. It means you are addressing your own work as much as the young people you support. Whilst you should not consider this in any way as a training, it will give you a start and make you feel confident and comfortable with exploring this work at a basic but crucial level.

So get ready, and cross the threshold now…

Part 1

The Core Sessions

Core Session 1
Nuts and Bolts

'The words are rooted with the breath.'

Cicely Berry

In this first core session we introduce the power of the voice, the basic breathing work, theory and practice, floor work, body awareness, feeling of ease/relaxation, listening, diction, vowels, tone and style, and singing. The class is fun, but is primarily technical and energetic. If you do it all, it should last about ninety minutes.

You do not have to follow this plan slavishly. It is what *I* do, and you will have your own style. In addition, you might want to shift components around depending on the nature of your group, to say nothing of the venue, how much time you have, the participants' backgrounds and whether you are working in a youth theatre, school or college. I will give guidance, but these adjustments are up to you. I think if it if it suits your group, you could stand to use this same plan for a few sessions with just a different poem to work on at the end.

If ninety minutes is too long then split the session into two. If you are more inclined to start with short sessions you might go straight to the micro sessions in Part 3, and come back to these longer sessions. However, these first two sessions are the bedrock of the work, so if you can, start here.

You need to take your time if you are new to the work. You might feel that you yourself only feel confident enough to take a small piece of these sessions. That is okay too. Do not get too overfaced by all the explanations. Initially every exercise needs explaining to you with care and that takes space in the book. It does not take as long to do them!

The Room, the Warm-up Sheet and You

Ideally you must try and have a room which is light, airy, and big enough for people to move around in. Importantly, it needs to have a decent floor which is not too cold and which is clean and comfortable to lie on. If it isn't easy to lie on the floor you can try some of the breathing work in the *Qigong* standing position we explored in your own warm-up (but that is really a later stage of the work, so if you can manage to get the students lying on the floor, then do so). If you are in a gym there might be mats available. If not, perhaps they can be encouraged to bring in their own mat. As they are going to lie on the floor and do a lot of movement, people need to be in clothes that are, as they say, 'comfortable to move in'.

I have always supplied the participants at the end of the first session with a copy of a warm-up sheet they can do at home right from the start. If you do this, stress *regularity*; five minutes' practice a day is better than thirty minutes a week. Some of my home warm-up (printed at the back of the book and available to download on the Nick Hern Books website) involves them making sound, but they can do it silently if they are afraid how others may react. The important thing to stress initially is that they try and reintroduce the body to breathing diaphragmatically through the exercises. For the teacher/facilitator, this should be the most important goal initially with their work at home.

Maybe you will have done some of the exercises in the Introduction that day to prepare yourself, before you start with the group. It is important to remember that voice work more than any other theatre tool needs the body and mind as easy as possible, especially when you are starting out.

Part One: Starting the Session

Letting It Go

A good exercise for leaving the day behind.

- Begin by getting the group into a circle, and ask them simply to breathe and stand, feel their feet on the floor, and get a sense of where their body is uneasy or even tense. Have them bring their attention to that place, and say inside, just 'let go'. Ask them to close their eyes and get a sense of being in the room, to get a sense of where they are in the room, where the walls are, what it feels like to be in this circle with this group, their friends, to get ready to start on their drama session. To listen for sounds. To feel the atmosphere.

- Suggest they imagine that all around each of them is their day and their concerns of the day. Get them to imagine what these concerns look like. Are they buzzing around? Are they floaty? What? Is a thought grabbing onto them like some little creature? What does it feel like in their imagination?

- Everyone is going to step forward with their eyes closed and step out of that little atmosphere of their thoughts and concerns. Suggest they step forward and then leave the thoughts behind.

- Ask them to open their eyes. Look around at their friends and share their energy with them. It is okay to laugh or smile but not to talk. Ask them to notice if they feel differently.

- Ask them to turn back to their little atmosphere. With a big sweeping gesture and a shout, all together they sweep their thoughts and concerns away.

So now it is time to introduce the work. It is important you explain the importance of the voice, how much of the work is important not only for acting but for life itself, and how when you go on the stage you have pretty much yourself to work with. You are your instrument.

Ask: what are the things you need to speak clearly, and loudly for the stage? Explore the responses, but know that our first stop is going to be breathing...

Happy Birthday (1)

- Ask the group to breathe in deeply and sing 'Happy Birthday', and keep going without taking a breath. This might be hard for some. Tell them not to cheat by taking sneak breaths.

- Ask for feedback. What happens to the voice as the breath runs out? Answers might be... 'It gets quieter', 'It makes me tense', 'It sounds weak', 'It doesn't go anywhere'. So we need a lot of breath to power the voice. It is our fuel, and powers everything we do. Be aware that this might be the very first time this has occurred to them.

Some Theory

With the right groups the theory can be useful, upfront. With others it can be off-putting. You decide.

- Ask them to consider the moment before they go to sleep, how they let go and their breathing changes. You might find it useful here to explain the theory behind diaphragmatic breathing, which we went through in the Introduction. It can be useful to demonstrate the action of the diaphragm by using your arms, knitting your fingers together in a 'cradle' loosely together in front of your body. As you breathe in, the 'cradle' goes down, then as you breathe out, the 'cradle' rises.

- Tell the group that it was the way they breathed when they were born, that it is taught in relaxation classes all over the world and is fundamental to many disciplines, such as yoga, *Qigong*, etc. Explain that it is quite natural to feel challenged about changing your breathing behaviour. It is useful to reassure those who have been to singing class that they will notice a slight difference in the technique. Neither is wrong.

Please note: It is important to tell them that there will be a lot of physical work, and only *they* know whether they have any physical issues they need to take care of. They need to look after themselves, and come and explain afterwards if there is anything they have to avoid. You need to be very reassuring about this, because doing this work can create a lot of anxiety for some young people.

Part Two: Warm-up

I suggest you do all these exercises *with* the group. If you do them, they are less likely to be so nervous about doing them. The exercises I use are based on theatre training, yoga and t'ai chi. They are all leading up to the floor work.

General Tips

Firstly, a tip on *pace*. Once you start the stretches part of the warm-up, you can up the pace considerably if you feel it is necessary, to keep them interested. Ideally it is better to start slow, as it makes them more aware of their movement, and they are less likely to hurt themselves, but varying the pace can be helpful to retain their engagement.

Also, it is good to try and keep the energy focused between each exercise. Getting the young people to stand in neutral, arms by the sides, feet parallel, knees slightly bent, when they are not doing exercise, can stop a kind of 'flopping back' into their everyday concerns. This might be more of a long-term aim, I know, but it depends on the type of group and the setting.

Beach Ball

- Ask everybody to stand in the *Qigong* standing position (see the Introduction, page 16, for a fuller explanation): that is, feet parallel to shoulders, knees slightly bent, spine straight but not stiff, shoulders easy, head aligned with spine, looking ahead.

- Ask them to slowly lift their arms as if they are holding a large beach ball (about a metre across) to their chest. Watch for tension in their bodies. The most likely place is neck and shoulders. Suggest they consider that part of their body and say to themselves 'let go'.

- Next ask them to *breathe down*. To imagine they are breathing right into the soles of their feet. If they have a lot of chest and shoulder movement they are not to judge it, but notice it.

- Then ask them to breathe in and very gently, at the same time, to open up the arms.

- Then ask them to breathe out, bringing their arms back into the beach-ball position. Suggest they imagine a connection between the breath and the movement of the arms (x4).

- Ask them to bring their arms to their sides, then, as they breathe in, slowly raise them as if they are drawing an arc with their fingers, over the head. Their hands are palms up. Ask them, in the space between the in- and out-breath, to turn their hands so that the palms are down, then to breathe out and bring their arms in the same arc back to their sides (x4).

- Keeping a nice relaxation going, ask everyone to notice whether they feel differently from when they came in. (So much of this work is about teaching awareness.) Then tell them that the next exercise needs to be done with the same 'feeling of ease' with which they did this one. Ideally it is good to keep a sense of focus between the exercises if you can, so that you do not allow the concentration to slacken.

Easy Stretch

- Ask the group to knit their fingers together, and hold their hands in front of their chests; then, breathing in, ask them to turn their hands, and stretch up. As they breathe out, then need to bring the hands back to the starting position. Ask them to keep the stretches light (x4).

- Ask them to push their knitted hands out front and push the chest to the back. Try and get them to release tension, to let go (x4).

- Then ask them to reach down, hanging from the waist. Get them to breathe and let the weight of the body take the upper body further towards the floor. The legs should be straight and shoulder-width apart at least.

- All the time, ask them to *notice* their breath.

Puppets

- Ask everyone in their hanging-down positions to let go, releasing the knees, so they release the back further. They should go floppy and loose like puppets, bending over from their waists.

- Ask them to shake head and shoulders *only*, and let out a moaning sound. Do it for them so they are not embarrassed. Ask them to consider whether that is a freer sound.

- Then, *very slowly*, ask them to bring themselves to standing, curling up the spine vertebra by vertebra. The head and neck should be the last to lift into place.

Tip: Encourage slowness. Encourage them to notice where their backs come up in a lump rather than bit by bit.

Head Rolls

- Ask everyone to drop their heads to their chests and then *very slowly* roll them to the right, to the back, to the left and back to the front in a circle (x4 each way).

Tip: Tell them to check the jaw and shoulders especially for tension. These are two of the main areas which harbour it, so keep an eye out.

Shoulder Chugs and Rolls

- To vary the tempo a bit, so they do not go to sleep, give the instruction, 'Shoulders *up*, shoulders *centre*, shoulders *down*' (x4).

- Do this quite quickly, like a game. And smile. Enjoy it.

- Then rotate the shoulders forward very slowly, and incorporate the whole body almost like you were skiing in slow motion (x4). Then take the shoulders back in a circle the other way. Fully engage the knees and lower body (x4).

Hand Throwing

- Ask everyone to turn to the left and find someone to look at on the other side of the circle. Ask them to put their weight on the left foot and change their weight to the right foot, throwing their right hand as if they are throwing it to their partner. Ask them to count '1-2-3-4-5-6-7-8' aloud, sending the sound across to their partner. Do this vigorously. Turn the other way and repeat. This is a good releasing exercise.

- Now ask them to do exactly the same but this time not as loudly, but still to feel their voices are going to their partner. Try it one more time, this time throwing *silently*.

Tip: This is an important exercise for radiating/receiving (fully communicating across a space) and for projection. It emphasises the voice as something that you use to reach others with your emotions and ideas. It will be developed further; right now it is a fun game.

Also it is one of the exercises in which we are encouraging them to use their *whole body*. This is going to come up a lot. The more they and you can understand that the body can help you with clarity and expression, the fuller and more successful you will be.

Chest and Waist Isolations

- Get them to push *only* the chest forward, keeping the rest of the body still, then back. Forward and back (x4).

- Then slide the ribs from one side to the other (x4).

- Then try a full circle of the ribcage and chest (x4 each way).

- Then, keeping the hips to the front, swing the whole upper body to each side, arms loose, loosening the waist muscles (x4 each way).

Tip: The isolation of the chest and ribs to the side proves very difficult for a lot of people. Keep it light and fun. Get them to put their hands on their lower ribs and push against their hands first one way, then the other. No problem if they can't do it. Assure them it is tricky and takes practice. All of these exercises are simply to wake up their bodies, particularly in areas that are important for voice work.

Yoga Side-bend

- Breathe in as you lift the right arm up to the sky in parallel to the body (though not too stretched) and have the legs in a wide stance.
- Then bend over from the waist towards the left, as you breathe out.
- When you are as far over as you can go *without forcing it*, breathe in – and then, as you breathe out, let the weight of your body take you further. Take two more breaths, letting the out-breath take you further into the stretch. Don't force it.
- Then breathe in, come up, lower the right arm.
- Then lift the left arm and bend to the right and do the same thing again. Then breathe in and come up straight and lower the left arm.

Tip: If this is the first time they are doing this exercise, you should not be picky, but if you use it more regularly, check if anyone is sticking their hips out to the side and try to get them to correct it; also to keep the body all in the same plane in order to get the full benefit of the stretch. But that, too, might be for another day.

Hip Circles

- It is nice to make some slow hip circles, four each way. This way you have now come all the way down the upper body.

A fun variation is to do forward/back (x4) and side-to-side (x4) vigorously *before* you do the circles. It has a strong embarrassment quotient so it depends on where your group is at! It can be a good laugh.

Leg Throw

- Get the group to kick out with '*HA!*' then a '*HE!*' then a '*HO!*' Go faster each time. Try and get them to stay together (x8).

Balancing Act

Balance has an extremely important effect on our confidence, our contact with the earth, and our ability to speak clearly.

- Ask the group to stand on one leg, and try balancing. Get them to move their upper bodies as adventurously as they can whilst staying in balance.

- Suggest they try to change the tempo of the movement and really push their bodies. Get them to explore changing the tempo of their movements too.

- Then ask them to change legs and repeat.

Tip: This is a good place for you to notice where participants have tension. The introduction of tempo into the body is important, as later in our sessions we might start to consider how tempo affects speech and emotion.

Hey Hey Hee Hee Hah Hah

- Get them to do some jumps to flex their feet. Then, to take a wide stance. Look across the circle. Have someone in their sights! Start *slowly*.

- All point with the right arm, and call across to someone '*HEY!*'

- Then take out the right arm and put in the left and call across '*HEY!*'

- Then reach to the right sideways with the right arm and say '*HEE!*'

- Then reach to the left sideways with the left arm and say '*HEE!*'

- Then with the right arm you reach to the ceiling and say '*HAH!*'

- Then with the left arm you reach to the ceiling and say '*HAH!*'

- Then you start again from the beginning.

- Speed up as they get the hang of it.

- Do as many as you feel you want to.

This exercise can be as fast or as slow as you like. You can be as demanding as you feel appropriate (try and get people to really bend their knees, stretch and focus out beyond their hands, for instance).

Tip: It's a great exercise for ensemble, voice, and movement. Try and get the group to slow down if someone gets behind, and encourage those who are confused to keep trying to get back into the exercise.

Stretch and Yawn

- Ask the group to stretch and yawn, noticing how the throat relaxes and opens at the back when they do it. It is good to yawn if they are nervous before performing!

Song

You could end this section with a simple singing round. Do not be judgemental about whether people can sing or not. My policy is that everyone can sing simple tunes. Singing out of tune has two main causes. One is not enough breath and the other is not being able to listen.

Massage

Where you place this or whether you do it at all is down to you. Physical contact within a group is such a personal issue, but it is good to do this if you feel it is appropriate to your group.

- Ask the group to tighten the circle and turn to the right, then ask them to put their hands on the shoulders of the person in front. This will involve a lot of giggling and moving around. Tell them that if they have trouble reaching the person in front to step in towards the middle of the circle, so everyone can reach each other's shoulders comfortably.

- Now ask them to massage the shoulders of the person in front. Ask them to go down as far as the bottom of the shoulder blades. Ask them to massage how they want, but to remember they are serving the person in front of them and the person being massaged controls the process. This is very important.

- After a squeezing massage, then repeat with a patting motion of the same area, and then a washing down with the flats of the hands, using them like big paintbrushes.

- Then, one by one, get each young person to raise the shoulders of the person they have been massaging. Tell the one whose shoulders are being lifted to let the person lifting do the work. Let them try it three times each. Do not make the people whose shoulders are tense feel awkward. Reassure them that this is all part of a process of finding out about where tension is in their body and how they can deal with it.

Tip: If you work with this, take special care at the moment one person lifts the other's shoulders. Get the lifter to put their hands on the person's arms first, and stay there for a second so the lifter gets used to them. Ask the person whose shoulders are being lifted to say 'let go' to themselves and then get the other person to lift. This can often stop the person whose shoulders are being lifted from tensing up.

Part Three: Floor Work and Breathing

1.

2.

3.

We now reach what I feel is really the most important part of the work of these early sessions. Ask all the young people to lie on their backs on the floor. Lying on the floor can be a *massive* issue for some young people, and, of course, it helps if the room is warm and the floor is clean. Issues such as a feeling of vulnerability, wearing inappropriate clothing, or having someone in your group watching and not participating can all be challenges. Mats can help a lot and making sure that young women are not wearing skirts, because they are going to be putting their feet flat on the floor and raising their knees. Should floor work be difficult at first, you might try and do this work standing with knees bent, or if even that is difficult, sitting upright (not slouched) in a chair.

In Figure 1 you will see a young person standing with knees bent and back straight. Both hands are on the belly. You can explore all the work from here, but the back and pelvis do not have the same degree of relaxation, and the young person can be more easily distracted. On the other hand, some people feel quite threatened by lying on the floor so standing up might work better for them. In Figure 2 it is good if the chair can be the 'wrong' way round as it helps prevent slouching.

Assure them that this is an important part of the work where we are really going to practise and explore the breathing. It will be nice and easy. Highlight the usefulness of this part of the work in settling and easing stress. I am going to continue as if all are working from the lying position (Figure 3), because this is really the optimum position for this work.

Tip: Take as much time as you feel you can, without them disengaging. You will get more of a sense of this as you use these exercises more. If you feel the group is ready, try these floor exercises for a few sessions. I find that many young people look forward to them as a moment of relaxation in their session and in the week.

Relaxation and Awareness Procedure

- Ask the group to feel their bodies on the floor, to be really *in* their bodies. Notice if they feel any tension there. If so, where is it? Direct their attention to it and ask them to say in their heads 'let go', and their tense body part will let go. Tell them that if there is any residue from the tension of the day left in their bodies, they might like to think of it just seeping into the floor.

- Ask them to stretch their bodies along the floor with their hands on the floor above their heads – a stretch which goes from the tips of the fingers to the tips of the toes. Then let the stretch go. Encourage them again to use the phrase 'let go' as they relax (x4).

- Get them to lift their feet up gently, bring their knees up and put the soles of their feet flat on the floor, so their spines are almost fully on the floor. Tell them not to worry if their backs are not fully on the floor.

- Say you are going to ask them to 'breathe in for four, hold in for four, breathe out for four'. As they breathe in, they should curl their lower back upwards, bringing their hips off the floor. On *hold*, they stay there, and on the *out*-breath they bring the pelvis gently down. Do this three times, each time asking the student to curl more of the spine, and hence bring their hips further off the floor.

Tip: it is particularly important that they 'police' themselves in this exercise if they have any back problems.

- Ask them to raise their shoulders from the floor, and when you click your fingers, they let them fall (x4).

- Then ask them to slightly raise their hands from the sides of their bodies, you click your fingers and they let them go (x4).

- Ask them to move their heads easily and gently from side to side. After a few seconds ask them to bring their heads back to centre.

- Now ask them to focus on the face. Imagine the jaw hinge melting then the spot between the eyebrows softening.

Tip: Walk around and check if anyone's head sits uncomfortably on the floor, head back and chin out would the most extreme. This can be due to tension down the spine, in the shoulders and/or the neck. In this case, take a small book with about an inch spine, get them to lift their heads a little and slide it under. This prevents discomfort and aligns the spine. If the tension is severe you might need a thicker book. A person may have to use a book each time they work on the floor if this is an issue for her.

Breathing Exercises (1): Basic Breath

- Ask them to place their hands on their tummies, remembering this is the belt line and *not* the ribs. Go round and look at the position of their hands. The point is that if they have their hands over the lower ribcage, they will imagine they are using their diaphragms when they are not. High positioning of the hands encourages them to breathe higher into their chests.

- Ask them to feel the breath streaming in through the nose down into the lungs and *as if* it is going right into the belly. This will make the tummy fill up, and the hands rise. You might want to explain what is really happening here (see the Introduction, page 13), but I think that if you want to explain it, then you are better to do it earlier, or certainly separately. What we are asking them to do is learn by practice and experience, not by intellectualising.

- Now ask everyone to very, *very* gently pull the stomach in and let the air out of the mouth. Allow just the sound of the air to come from the lips. Imagine that the air has been on this journey from the atmosphere, then deep into the lungs and, imaginatively at least, down into the belly. Spend a few minutes with this, breathing in and out. Check out how people are doing.

- Ask them to imagine the rhythm of the ocean, emphasising the out-breath as the 'tide' goes out.

- If they feel any tension as the breath makes its journey, ask them to locate where it is. Bring their attention to that place,

43

feel the tension and then tell the tense place, just 'let go'. It is important to use sound on the out-breath rather than text, as even the most innocent sentence might send the body running back to its regular way of breathing and the tensions that go with it.

• Now ask them to breathe into the belly for four (you count) hold in for four, and then to let go, and this time to voice the sound quietly (x4). Encourage them to take more breath and push the tummy muscles in a little harder (that is, make a little more noise each time). Do not allow them to shout though. They are making a vocal sigh, almost a moan.

Breathing Exercises (2): More Fuel for the Body

Explain to them that as they discovered when they tried to sing 'Happy Birthday' on one breath (page 30) they discovered it was absolutely crucial to have plenty of breath. Less breath means they are more likely to hurt their voices when they are rehearsing, and this is every bit as important in a naturalistic play as it is in Shakespeare or something more stylised.

• Ask them to breathe in for four, hold for four, out for four (x2).

• Then breathe in for six, hold for six, out for six (x2).

• Then breathe in for eight, hold for eight, out for eight (x2).

• Now ask them to fix on a spot on the ceiling and imagine the breath is going right down into the belly, the tummy muscles are pushing and the sound is coming from their mouths like a golden fountain of sound, out to the spot on the ceiling. This visualisation of a golden sound can work well. Tell them they are going to make the sound '*mmmmmmAAAAH*'. You need to assure them that this might take a bit of practice and not to be despondent or dismissive. You are trying to get them to explore the connection between the belly, breath and sound here. Make sure they do a substantial '*mmmmmm*' before they open out the sound (x4).

- If most of them seem to have it, then ask them to sing 'Helloooooooooooooo.'

Tip: Notice if anyone changes their breathing when you ask them to speak a word. It is amazing how the regular habit kicks in, often instantly, as soon as regular speech is introduced. If you feel this is happening with a few in the group then stay with sound.

- When they have completed these first floor exercises, ask them to roll onto their side, stay in that position for a few seconds and then get up *slowly*. The body can sometimes be overwhelmed by the amount of oxygen a person takes in when breathing diaphragmatically and they might need to take their time getting up.

- You might ask them if they have any questions at this point. Ask them what it feels like, and if there is anything they feel they need explaining again. If you are instructing here and are looking to get them to develop this work, rather than simply giving them an experience, you might suggest at this point that this is what they could do to practise, if only for a few minutes each day.

Part Four: Core Voice Awareness, Diction and Resonance

Find the Sound (1)

- Ask them to close their eyes. Try and keep the focused mood going if you can. Explain to them that the sensitivity of the voice is enhanced by how much we really *listen*, and this is a game for listening. Maybe ask them for a second to listen to the sounds outside, then the sounds in the room, and finally the sound of their own breathing.

- Explain that every person in the room is going to sing a '*mmmmmaaaaaahhhhhh*' sound. They can breathe whenever they like but they need to keep the sound going and keep their eyes closed.

- Make sure everyone has their eyes closed. This can be hard for some, so suggest they put a hand over their eyes if they have any trouble. While you are talking, you walk around the room. You explain that you are going to touch someone on the shoulder. When every person starts to make the '*mmmmmaaaaaahhhhhh*' sound, the person you have touched will instead sing a '*mmmmmeeeeeeeeeee*' sound. So everyone but one person will be singing '*mmmmaaaah*', and one person will be singing '*mmmmmeeeeeeeeeee*'.

- The job of the '*maaaaahs*' is to find the '*meeeee*' with their eyes closed. Once the '*meeeee*' is found (the '*meeeee*' can also move around as well) anyone who finds her then needs to stay with her and change her own sound to '*mmmmmeeeeeeeeeee*'. Eventually the whole room is full of people hanging on to each other singing '*mmmmmeeeeeeeeeee*'.

- Once all are together, tell them you are going to clap your hands and everyone must open their eyes and keep the sound going. When they open their eyes, they will want to relax and giggle. Try and control that because it destroys the energy. If it happens, stop the exercise here. No problem – we will develop it later.

- If it does work okay, call a name and they must, with eyes open, lead and change the sound and add a repetitive movement that goes with the sound; then all must follow; then call another who changes the sound and movement and all follow her; then another. Finally one more, and ask that person to bring the movement and sound to a close. All stop together.

Sound Circle

- Leading on from this, with everyone in a circle, tell them you are going to lead with a sound and a movement. Let's say you make a '*fffffuh*' sound and push with your hands out into the centre, try and engage the whole body. For the first time you do this, start energetically. It is easier for people to engage energetically – don't be subtle.

Tip: Engaging the whole body gives the way you move a major impact on the voice. This is the whole theory behind Chekhov's Psychological Gesture.

- The whole group will copy your movement – and not just the movement but also the energy, pace and feeling of it. Once everyone has got it, explain that the person on your right must change your movement (using it to find some kind of *inspiration* for it). In other words, they cannot do any movement they feel like, they have to base it on yours. You might need to demonstrate a possibility; for instance, your forthright '*ffffuh*' with its strong pushing motion, might lead on to a scattering motion and a sound of '*chhhhhaaaa*' from the next leader.

- Once the second person has led and the person on *their* right feels the whole group has the '*chhhhaaaa*' movement and feeling, then *that* person starts to lead with a new movement inspired by the one before, and the whole group follows her movement. This change of leader continues until you have gone round the whole group, maybe twice.

Tip: This exercise is to encourage the connection between voice and body. It is fun and energetic, and again an exercise you can develop further. Try and get them to make the movement as full and energised as you can.

Diction Warm-up

Without clear diction it is impossible to hear what someone is saying, and if you can't hear what they are saying you are not going to want to listen to them in the theatre. Suggest to them how important it is to be clear when they are working, or doing presentations in school or college; that this work has many more uses.

This section is probably the nearest you might get to the stereotypical assumptions of a speech and drama class but I would advise you to keep it physical, strong and fun.

- *Shampoo*. Ask them to massage their scalps vigorously as if they are washing their hair (for young people who just did their hair this can be challenging!). Get them to massage into their necks too and even the shoulders a little.

- *Massage the jaw*. It might help for them to re-imagine the melting of the hinge of the jaw we did earlier.

- *Rinsing*. With hands on the face, get them to draw down their hands vigorously as if they were getting water off it Get them to make a '*fuh*' sound as they do it (x4).

- *Blow through the lips* (twenty seconds). Really loosen the lips.

- *Tongue flicking*. Flick out your tongue like a lizard (x4).

- *Chew fast/chew slow*. The change of tempo is good. Again, it reminds the whole being how different a feeling a new pace can give you.

- *Tongue circles.* Circle the tongue each way with the tongue on the outside of the teeth (x4). Then repeat, but this time on the *inside* of the teeth (x4).

- *Tongue directions.* Tongue to your nose/to your chin (x4).

- Tongue across side to side (x4).

- *Rubber face.* Put your fists in front of your face, then, as if you are stretching the face, pull the fists apart and stretch the face horizontally like a rubber mask. Bring your hands together, then pull them vertically and stretch the face vertically. Now try on the diagonal, both ways.

- Rinse the face again to finish.

T–L–D

- '*Tttt*' – '*llll*' – '*dddd*'. These are all tip of the tongue exercises. Do each one three or four times, e.g. '*tttt tttt tttt tah*' (x4), Then '*llll llll llll lah*' (x4), etc.

- Then '*tttt llll dddd*' (x6).

- Then '*tttt llll dddd, llll dddd tttt, dddd tttt llll*' – imagine they're written in front of you, if that makes it easier (x4).

- Do '*bbbb kkkk*'. Notice how with '*buh*' the sound is focused at the front of the mouth. '*Kuh*' is at the back of the mouth. Try '*pppp*' and '*gggg*' similarly.

- Ask them to do '*buh duh guh*'/ '*puh tuh kuh*', slowly at first to register the focus, and then speed up.

Try:

'*Izun-zana – DO-ra-DO.*'

'*BET-a-TOOra – Catcha – TOO.*'

'*METa TARSa TARTal-MEEna.*'

'*Tar mel ZIN ZAN ZUN*' (it is a rhyme about a bee!).

Tip: For these basic but crucial exercises, I cannot overemphasise how important it is to get them to use their bodies as much as you can. It enlivens and changes the sound, often getting them to speak in ways they had never considered.

You need to lead. What I mean is, if you say '*tuh*' with a punch, it is different to how you will say it if you glide your hand slowly across your body at the same time. Get them to experiment with this, at the same time as getting them to speak the sounds clearly. Keep it rhythmic and fun. Do the sounds with them, or with call and answer (you say them, they repeat).

Resonance (1)

Before you start this series of exercises, you might explain that the more resonant the voice is, the less effort is needed for your voice to carry, the more interesting it sounds, the more powerful it will be, and the more you as a performer will be able to share your feelings and those of the character. Explain that the whole body is like an instrument to be played. Do these exercises with them.

- Move the hand to the top of the head. Breathe in. Focus on where the hand is and send the sound up there. Hum into the hand. Try and make the hand vibrate, with a '*MMMMMMMAAAAHHH*'. Direct the vibration there.

- Put the hand to the bridge of the nose. Breathe in. Hum into the hand. Try and make the hand vibrate, with a '*MMMMMMMAAAAHHH*'. Direct the vibration there.

- Put your fingers lightly to your lips. As you breathe out and start to hum, bring your hand from your lips to about a foot in front of you. Open the sound '*MMMMMMMAAAAHHH*'. Focus on the hand as if you were singing into a microphone.

- Now put the hand on the chest. Breathe in. Hum into the hand. Try and make the chest vibrate, with a '*MMMMMMMAAAAHHH*'. Direct the vibration there.

- Now ask them to see if they can direct the resonance into any of those four places, to move their hands and the sounds around; to play with '*MMMMMMMAAAAHHH*'. They breathe when they need to. Ask them what they notice. Where do *they* resonate best?

Happy Birthday (2)

This game is a good break from a workshop which has been fairly focused.

- Make it someone's birthday. Put the group into teams of four or five. Each group is going to work on singing 'Happy Birthday' in a different style and present to the group. One group might choose a boy band, one a hip-hop group, one an opera, one a dance track, one a choir. They have to 'stage' this as well. This exercise will certainly take about ten to fifteen minutes in a session if you have a new group.

- After they have shown the exercise to each other, which is usually very good fun, discuss what they found out about the voice. Did they find they sang in a certain way? What was the quality of singing that way? This exercise explores amongst other things how you can transform something by the way in which you vocalise it and present it.

Tip: With this kind of exercise, where they have to prepare and present, it is useful to get people to work fast, and not spend too much time talking. What they lose in accuracy, they gain in spontaneity. It also stops them being over-intellectual. How often we see young people discussing for hours and not getting up and doing! Make sure also, if the group is new to you, that everyone is being included. Later I will talk further about my feelings on criticism and development.

Part Five: Exercises in Communication and a Piece of Text

It is very important in any short course to give people an idea of where this is going *practically*, especially when the work is fairly new to them, and our final set of exercises is to do with one of the principal purposes of speech: *communication*.

Throwing the Ball (1)

In a circle, the group is going to mime throwing and catching a ball to each other. This is a Chekhov exercise and, though not primarily a vocal exercise, that is what we are using it for here.

Tip: The reason we mime the ball is that playing with a real one always brings up a wealth of childhood horrors, and you have to spend a long time practicing and reassuring people. You do not have that time. When people drop a real ball there is a dissipation of energy you do not need at this stage. The *way* we throw is important. The student must have one foot behind the other and be able to throw underarm with an easy swing.

- Start the 'throwing'. When people 'throw' it is important they stay with their throwing arm extended, looking at the person they are throwing to and sending their energy towards them. They are sustaining the movement. This is important as the student can feel both that the movement is finished and that they have sent energy to the catcher. (More on what that means exactly in the next session.)

- The person who 'catches' must receive the 'ball' looking at the thrower, so an exchange is made. Then the thrower can return to their regular stance. Do not initially go too fast. Keep it smooth and steady. Practise and be precise with these movements. It might be easier, depending on the nature of the group, to work externally with the mechanics of the movement, rather than talking about sending your energy. People are often very reluctant to stay with their arm outstretched, they 'throw' their energy out quickly and weakly. Point out how, on stage, it is vitally important to share and communicate with the other actors as well as the audience.

- Ask them to add a sound when they throw. Let them use their own name, for example. Get them to notice when they feel their voices do not reach their catcher. Explore for a second the *why* of that. Could it be they need more breath to project effectively?

Is There Anybody There?

I use poetry a lot. It is good for voice work because you do not have to worry too much about character – it is more about what the words do for you, how they make you feel, and what the atmospheres and ideas are. Poems also tend to be a more manageable length.

Use a fairly simple and evocative poem, for instance, 'The Listeners' by Walter de la Mare, reproduced below. Whatever you choose to work with, let it be a good poem, as there is little point in the group using poor material. I would say this about all the texts you might use.

Tip: Remember, when you use text, if it is going to be a regular thing, to make a routine where people can take next week's poem, speech or scene home the week before. Many young people have reading issues, or have English as a second language, and it helps to have got to know the text beforehand.

'The Listeners' by Walter de la Mare

'Is anybody there?' said the Traveller,
Knocking on the moonlit door;
And his horse in the silence champed the grasses
Of the forest's ferny floor:
And a bird flew up out of the turret,
Above the Traveller's head:
And he smote upon the door a second time;
'Is there anybody there?' he said.
But no one descended to the Traveller;
No head from the leaf-fringed sill
Leaned over and looked into his grey eyes,
Where he stood perplexed and still.
But only a host of phantom listeners
That dwelt in the lone house then
Stood listening in the quiet of the moonlight
To that voice from the world of men:
Stood thronging the faint moonbeams on the dark stair,

That goes down to the empty hall,
Hearkening in an air stirred and shaken
By the lonely Traveller's call.
And he felt in his heart their strangeness,
Their stillness answering his cry,
While his horse moved, cropping the dark turf,
'Neath the starred and leafy sky;
For he suddenly smote the door, even
Louder, and lifted his head: –
'Tell them I came, and no one answered,
That I kept my word,' he said.
Never the least stir made the listeners,
Though every word he spake
Fell echoing through the shadowiness of the still house
From the one man left awake:
Ay, they heard his foot upon the stirrup,
And the sound of iron on stone,
And how the silence surged softly backward,
When the plunging hoofs were gone.

- Read the poem in the circle with each person reading one line in turn. Don't be disheartened if everything sounds dead. Part of our job is to get young people over the hurdle of speaking text so that what they find in the exercises can flow into it. That takes time.

- Ask them to memorise that line if possible and the line of the person who comes before them so they know when to speak. Try the whole poem through a couple of times so that everyone can do it without the text, if possible.

- Now in the circle, get them to speak their lines in order with the feeling they are telling a story. They are all telling the story to each other.

- Once they have got that, you might like to use an imaginative key, like, 'Imagine you are sitting by a fire in a cosy house and the wind is howling...' Try the poem again. You might try, 'Imagine there is a cold, dark, threatening atmosphere, like a prison.' Give them really time to imagine these settings. Try again.

One of the keys to this sort of exercise is to build up slowly. By the time you are giving imaginative suggestions like this, the poem should be starting to sound more alive.

If that has gone well, you might split them into two groups and have them perform to each other.

Showing the Poem

- If you have time, and you need at least twenty or thirty minutes, split the group into two and get them to stage half of the poem each.

'The Listeners' is very clear, spooky and evocative, so is a good choice. (If I have a workshop around Hallowe'en it is always a big success!) By 'stage it', what I mean is they are going to speak their half of the poem and, as they do, they act it out, either literally or symbolically. This is good because it starts them thinking about what the poem means to them and the pictures it creates in their mind. Tell them also they must all speak some part of the poem.

- In their groups, as a starter, you might like to suggest they close their eyes and imagine they are *in* the world of the poem. What are the prevailing atmospheres and feelings that come up for them as they immerse themselves in this poetic world? These are the feelings and atmospheres they want to communicate to us, as well as the story. Ask them to compare feelings and pick one prevailing atmosphere they all want to go for and use that as their base line.

Pointers on Devising and Facilitating Presentation

Do not let them discuss too much. Breaking the habit of too much talk is difficult, but getting up on your feet means you can try out more options. The most important thing for the facilitator/teacher is that they *explore* in addition to just presenting. With poetry they might want to set 'who says what' first but once they have done it, persuade them to get up. They can change what they have set as they go, so their vision of how it looks enhances how they say it.

Let them explore isolating words or repeating them for effect if they like, as long as the spine of the story is clear and they are using the language.

As this is an early workshop, do not do too much critiquing. But do not be under the illusion that no critiquing is good as a rule. It depends on your group. When people are enthusiastic about theatre, they generally want to *learn*. We will talk more about critiquing later. Maybe say one thing that was good, one that needed improving. If you have time you might attempt to try out an improvement.

Always make sure that, when presenting, they *start from stillness* and give their piece a moment at the end. This shows a respect for their own work and for their audience.

Part Six: Ending the Session

I think having a strong ending to the session sends the participants out wanting more. It is really good to end positively. I think it is useful for us to remember we have led them through an *experience* as well as hopefully having taught them something.

You need to actively participate in either of the following games.

Song Circle

This is one of the most magical exercises I know. I learned it when in a production during an actor-led warm-up. Here are the rules.

- Form a circle. Tell the group that when you have finished talking, you all are going to hold hands and close your eyes.

- You will lead. You are going to sing a line, possibly a line from the piece you have been working on. ' "Is there anybody there?" said the Traveller,' is a good one, and it should not be longer than that. You will sing the line the same way over and over, and make the tune *easy*. If possible, try leaving a bar of four beats between the end of the sung line and the beginning of the next one, so there is a silent space.

- The group, with their eyes closed, will sing the same line with you. Everyone keeps going. Gradually, if anyone has the desire, they can start to harmonise on the original tune. They can use pieces of the line or single words if they want and put them into the empty bar. All being well, something quite magical can happen, and something quite intricate can develop. (If it doesn't the first time you try this, then keep at it. All you need in the group is one or two good singers to make it sound exciting.)

- *Everyone* must sing. If there is someone who right now feels they can't sing, tell them to stay with the base line, which you should not leave. If that is hard for them, suggest they speak or whisper the line in rhythm. This can sound great over the singing.

- If you feel anyone in the group might not keep their eyes closed, you might open your own, and notice who cannot manage to keep their eyes closed. You might want to follow this up later, reinforcing that it is important to commit to the exercises to get the full benefit and enjoyment from them.

- You must judge when to stop. Do give it enough time to catch fire! On the other hand you don't want them getting giggly, and making the end of the session disruptive. When you feel it is time to stop (and you need to explain this before you start) you will squeeze the hand of the person on your right. They will squeeze the hand of the person on their right and so on, so the squeeze goes round the circle. When you feel the squeeze come back to you, you know everyone knows. Tell them that when they get 'the squeeze', it does not mean, 'Oh great, it's over,' it means they have to listen and bring the music down slowly. When everyone has stopped singing and there are a few seconds' silence, you let go of the hands, open your eyes and clap. All applaud each other and the session is ended.

The Golden Hoop

This is a beautiful Michael Chekhov exercise, which does not employ voice, but you might feel is more appropriate for your group.

- Everyone stands in a circle. You suggest to them: 'We are going to imagine in front of us that there is a large golden hoop almost as big as this circle we are in, on the floor. In it is all the promise, learning and excitement of the workshop.'

- You need to explain and *show* them this first. As you do it you say: 'When someone wants to bend down slowly and pick up the hoop, the whole group goes down with them. We all pick up the hoop together. When everyone is standing with the hoop at their waists, a moment is taken for everyone to look around at everyone in the circle. Feel that moment. All together we will slowly throw the hoop up into the air like a balloon and watch it float away.'

- Having demonstrated, you then as a group do the exercise. Try not to be the person who instigates the movement, as though at the beginning you might have to be. When you have sent up the hoop stay staring at it for a moment, and then bring the arms down slowly.

- Say 'Thank you.'

At the very end of the session you might suggest they take a warm-up sheet for practice if you think it is appropriate. Suggest they focus on breath work.

This workshop is designed to introduce a whole range of fundamentals around using our voices, and something of an ethos towards working in this area with young people. Do not be too hard on yourself if you feel you did not achieve everything you set out to do, and reflect on what worked well. There is probably more here than you need for ninety minutes, so do not use the text work if you do not feel it is appropriate. Split the session up if you need to.

When teaching another session, do not be afraid of repetition. In some ways make a feature of it. There is a feeling, with youth work especially, that everything has to be new all the time; this is not always the case. This feeling of ritual through repetition is incredibly important and will encourage the young person to practise the voice work themselves at home.

In the next workshop we look at following on from this basic work with another session that expands the concerns of this one, before we move on to our shorter themed sessions.

Core Session 2
Imagine!

'I am certain of nothing but... the truth of
imagination.'

John Keats

This is a workshop plan that continues the work we did with the
group in Core Session 1. We will develop several exercises
explained earlier, which you may use to take your group further
and troubleshoot physical and vocal tension. As with the previous workshop plan it is roughly ninety minutes.

If I think an exercise needs repeating, I will indicate its place in
the last session. In addition to the basic exercises and floor work
we will now focus more on connecting the voice and breath to
the body using the *imagination*. They require a degree of matu-
rity and comfort with the work and between the group
members. School groups and groups with a primarily social
focus could be challenged by some of this session, therefore you
may need to be selective in the exercises you choose or wait
until your group is further down the road in terms of getting to
know each other.

In spite of the reservations above, it seems to me we have an
educational responsibility to work with the imagination, and
that should not stop when our young people reach secondary-
school level. Much of this work is about how the imagination
and body are a springboard for tone, feeling and emphasis; as a
result it will involve a little more risk-taking.

You might like to stick with the earlier plan in Core Session 1 for a while, or just cherry-pick one or two of these exercises – it's up to you.

Part One: Starting the Session

It is always good to use the *Letting It Go* exercise (page 29). As I am sure you know yourself, it can be hard to let go when you come into a class, particularly if you have a lot on your mind. Even as an adult, until you are in the atmosphere of the session and focused, you can want to run away and do something else.

Letting It Go (Variation)

If you feel the atmosphere is tense, unsettled or sluggish, you might want to use a more vigorous beginning.

- Ask the group to walk around the room. Ask them not to talk but to sense their bodies and how they are feeling right now. Is there a place where they are feeling tense (often shoulders or tummy), some part of the body which is saying, 'I would much rather be elsewhere'? Connect everything in your body up to that place of tension and start to move your limbs and throw it away. Just acknowledge the feeling. This is a great tension dispeller as people start to thrash about a bit. Encourage them to let it go vocally as well.

- Let it go on for about a minute and then bring the group to a circle.

Flyback

The *Flyback* is a process where we review what we did in the previous session. Often you can get people to do this physically, asking a member of the group to show an exercise to the others, but right now just get them to review the last session by telling you. Ask the question, 'What did you find out?' Try not to let them get away with saying, 'Breathing.' Get them to express what it is about breathing they remember. I find people use these labels a lot, as if the label gets them off the hook to express any feeling or discovery about it. You are trying to get them to express something deeper, more specific. Fill in the gaps with a few details of your own.

It is useful to remind them about breathing theory here. See if they remember it. Ask them if they remembered to notice when they were falling asleep how their breathing changed. Ask them if they managed to do any practice. I never haul anyone over the coals if they haven't, but I do explain that they will really improve if they can find even a little bit of time to do it.

Part Two: Warm-up

I would keep the warm-up pretty much as it is in the Core Session 1 (starting on page 31). You are just loosening the whole body, together as a group. It has a tribal, ritualistic feel, and gives the whole group a common focus.

Hey Hey Hee Hee Hah Hah (Development)

This exercise, also described in Core Session 1 (page 38), has two interesting developments:

- Try and get people to really bend their knees, stretch and focus beyond their hands, not only when they reach to someone across their circle, but also when they reach to the side and up. Ask them to imagine they are sending their energy far beyond their bodies. This is called radiating and we will return to it later.

- Another development, which is a fun game, is on the second 'HAH', you shout out a quality such as 'shyly'. When the group hears the word they say the whole next round of Hey Hey Hee Hee Hah Hah with a shy quality. They have to stay together but it completely changes the tone. At the next round on the second 'HAH' you may shout 'proudly,' and the whole group speaks the next round proudly, etc. Try 'greedily', 'angrily', 'fearfully', 'joyfully'. It also changes the way they move. This is especially good for getting groups to use their voices without having to speak alone.

Part Three: Floor Work and Breathing

The floor breathing work ought to be a staple part of all the sessions. Keep the programme the same as before, but now I would like to have a look at how you might help your group to deal with problems. However, do not feel you have to diagnose issues if you are not sure and only starting with this work.

Don't forget that you can always do this breathing work standing or sitting.

Floor Work: Troubleshooting

If you have experience with this work (and if you have done some observation exercises suggested in the Introduction) you will more than likely be able to spot tension in someone's body. Be sensitive to the fact that some may have spinal issues you do not know about.

Here are some common things to look out for:

- *General tension*: Fears of 'Am I doing this right?' 'This is stupid, why do I have to focus on breathing?' 'I hate lying on the floor' can create issues. You might spot this as a tense neck or hands. Perhaps you sense their jaw is tightened. The book under the head might be necessary (as discussed earlier), particularly if the head looks tilted upwards with the chin in the air. If you sense someone might be tense, and much of this sensing might be intuitive, gently reassure the young person that we are doing something we might do in many relaxation classes, or in yoga. If someone looks tense do not be afraid to ask them if they feel any tension. If they say yes, just get them to draw their attention to that point and then imagine something melting there. If the person says no it does not mean you are necessarily wrong but that there is no awareness of the tension. However, don't push it. If you see the person over a long time in your group keep an eye on this. Be reassuring at all times.

- *Throat and neck tension*: There could be tension here especially. Get them to swallow and yawn as much as possible and notice how the throat opens up. Keep checking in with them. 'Does that feel a bit better?' There is a strong chance they are closing up because they do not want to be loud. Maybe they are embarrassed or afraid. Ask them to focus on the tense spot and say 'let go' to themselves. This type of tension could have a long psychological history, as most tension does, and be a habit, so if you are familiar with your group, you need to gently and patiently keep reminding them.

- *Rib breathing (leading to tension in the chest)*: What you see is an inability to 'breathe down'. The shoulders rise a lot as they breathe in. If a person has done a lot of singing lessons, she may focus more strongly on the ribs. The problem is that if she does that, it provokes tension in all of the upper body and does not encourage her to breathe sufficiently when *speaking*. Make sure her hands *are* on the belt line, and get her to breathe 'under her hands' and push gently with her fingers. It might be helpful to get the whole group to lift their heads and shoulders off the ground, curling up the spine, like a sit-up. When the tummy muscles tighten, you emphasise that *that* is where the core and power of the breath comes from. Another way to emphasise the difference is this...

Finding the Belly Breath

- Ask the group to stand in pairs. Have one person stand behind the other and put their hands on the shoulders of the one in front.

- Ask the person in the front to bend their knees, keeping their feet shoulder-width apart and hands on their belt line. Ask them to try and breathe down. The person at the back needs to notice if the person's shoulders are lifting or not. If they are, ask the person at the back to put on a *little* pressure. This can be helpful in getting the person in front to breathe down. Swap over.

• Next, get Person One to breathe down, with their hands on the belly as they would do if they were doing the breathing exercises on the floor. Once fully inhaled, Person Two does a *very* slow motion 'punch' to the others' hands, helping to push in the tummy of Person One. Ask Person One to imagine they are being punched, and slowly double over. This is a great way to give people a sense of the tummy movement and that it is that movement of the belly, along with the quantity of breath, which makes a sound happen.

Part Four: Core Voice Awareness, Diction and Resonance

Find the Sound (2)

- Play as you did in *Find the Sound* (1) (page 45).

- When you get to the final part of the game (when everyone is together and making the same sound) call a name. That person must, with eyes open, lead and change the sound and add a repetitive movement that goes with that sound; then all must follow that leader.

- Then call another who changes the sound and movement and all follow her, then another. Finally, one more, and this time ask that person to change the *rhythm* and start to travel round the room with everyone making the same sound and movement and following the new leader. If it is going well, keep them moving round the room with a new leader.

- Ask the new leader to call someone and a new person leads the group and so on.

Tip: If you play this a few times over several sessions, start to get them to be aware that changes of pace, direction and sound can make their work interesting and varied. Always making the same kind of sound is unexciting and they need to have fun and find variety with it.

Encourage them to use consonants as well as vowel sounds and make a connection between how they move and the energy of the sound they make.

Diction Development and Resonance: Consonant Characters

This exercise can be very successful and emphasises the connection between body and voice.

- After the general diction work, ask the group to find their own space and tell them you are going to say a consonant, let's start with *'puh'*. Everyone is going to say *'puh'* and keep saying it. Ask them how it makes them feel, and let the body go with the sound; in other words, they start to be the character of 'puh'. This is quite easy and nowhere near as 'out there' as it sounds. Get them to do this at the same time and work on their own or they might get giggly, and when they feel more comfortable, they can have a 'puh' party and relate to each other! Let them play with each sound for about half a minute at least.

- Then change the sound to 'guh', 'vuh', 'buh', 'suh', 'ruh'. Get them to let the body and the sound work together. Say that will happen naturally if they don't think about it too much.

Tip: Try and get them to forget about thinking when they are exercising. This is very hard because our whole education is pro-grammed primarily towards thinking. If they listen to their bodies with a feeling of ease, then the sound will likely come out clear and true. They can think about it afterwards!

Part Five: Imagination Exercises

The Ideal Centre

I am repeating the instructions of this exercise on the *Ideal Centre* as described by Michael Chekhov, which was in your *own* practice (Introduction, page 19) – but for convenience I shall describe it again here. The Ideal Centre work is wonderful for well-being and wholeness. It is essential for projection of the voice even though it isn't a voice exercise as such. As you describe the imaginative journey give the group time to imagine. Do not rush. Repeat phrases now and then.

- Ask your group to stand with their knees slightly bent, feet firmly on the floor, to close their eyes and feel the energy of the earth beneath their feet. Suggest their legs are reaching into the earth like the roots of a tree.

- Ask them to imagine the energy of the earth beneath their feet as golden, benign and moving, full of potential, full of power. Then suggest they feel that same energy in their bodies: warm energy coming up through the soles of the feet and moving through the whole body. Ask them to feel that it is energy not only in the body but also coming from it, and suggest they stay with that feeling for a moment.

- Now ask them to imagine the sun is in the chest, strong and warm. To imagine that it is the centre from which all impulses come. Movements. Thoughts. Feelings. Ask them to try not to force this nor to think. Imagine that this warm heart centre is there, easily and totally accessible. If they lose it, tell them not to worry; just ask them to re-establish it in the imagination.

- Ask them to focus on the middle fingers and take the mind on a journey from there to the warm chest centre, through palms, wrists, forearms, elbows, upper arm, shoulder and then across the chest to the centre. Then focus on the ends of the big toes and take the mind on a journey up through the feet, ankles, calves, knees, thighs, pelvis, belly and spine up to the golden centre.

- Suggest they try, with eyes closed, to move the arms from that centre and open them wide as they breathe out. When the arms are wide, ask them to open the eyes and imagine the warm centre is filling the whole room. Bring the arms down and see if you can retain that imagination/sensation.

- Invite them to explore the sense that this energy is beaming out from the face, especially the eyes; tell them not to force it though, just imagine it. If a person feels the sensation is waning, suggest she just goes back to imagining the sun centre and the connection to it and it will return.

- Ask each person to share their energy with every single person in the room. Look at them. If someone gets a bit giggly it is okay, but ask them to be aware of an interplay of energy between the members of the group. Tell them this is called 'Radiating and Receiving'. It is the basis of all real communication.

- Ask how they feel. Ask them to try and maintain the Ideal Centre for the next exercise.

Throwing the Ball (2)

You might like to reintroduce *Throwing the Ball* here (page 52).

- Make sure the form of the mimed throw is right by running through both throwing and catching. Check that after they have thrown to their partner, who is receiving, they stay with their arm and body extended for a moment, really connecting to the 'catcher' (just as they do at the end of the *Ideal Centre* exercise when they are sharing their energy).

- Introduce a sound with the throw, then the name of the person, then 'Hello!' Ask if they feel their voice is reaching the catcher, and if not, what do they think might be the reason? (Breath is usually the answer, tension in the throw, or lack of focus.)

Tip: Remember to be very affirmative when the sound appears to reach the catcher! You are asking people to work on quite a deep level in a way that is new to them. They might well learn massively from someone else doing the exercise well.

Blue Voice, Green Voice

Returning to the *Ideal Centre* exercise, get everyone to find their own space and close their eyes. Get them to feel themselves in the moment: ask them to feel the earth beneath their feet and their body full of golden energy. Breathe in through the nose and out through the mouth.

- Now ask them to imagine they have a centre in their belly which is *dark blue* and that their whole body is full of dark-blue energy. As they breathe out through their mouth, dark blue comes out. Ask them to really feel that: feel what it is like to have dark-blue breath and get them to make their breath audible.

- Then ask them to voice that blue sound. You might have to count down to a 'Go!' to set them off. Try and get them to simply say their name with that blue voice. If that goes well, try:

- 'It is spring, moonless night in the small town' (Dylan Thomas, *Under Milk Wood*). Have them repeat this line a few times.

- Then get them to take a breath in and shake out the whole body. This helps them to shed whatever the imagination brought up for them when they were working. It helps them to let it go.

- Try the same process with *orange*: hopefully the sound will be different. Don't forget to say '1-2-3, Go!'

- Breathe in/shake out.

- Now with *silver.* Breathe in/shake out.

Tip: I always check in with them after this kind of exercise to find out how they felt. I feel this is important because this ability to play with your voice is empowering and they need to articulate and 'name' it. As Chekhov says, the brain is important but comes *after* you have experienced something. Also, when using the imagination exercises, it is important to breathe in and shake out, because this kind of work can be intense.

Soundtracks (1)

This is a game of which I take proud ownership, though I am sure someone was doing a version of it somewhere long before me. You need a big space for it. I have found it particularly successful with more mature devising groups, though others enjoy it too. It is energetic, so you need to have a good control of your group, and be doing it somewhere you can make lots of noise.

- Ask the group to go into pairs. (A three will work if necessary.) One of the pair is going to close her eyes (two if it's a three).

- The one with eyes open is going to make a soundtrack for the other person to move to. This sound can be anything except words. Variety needs to be encouraged, singing and rhythm (clapping or stamping) is allowed.

- The person with their eyes closed responds to the soundtrack and moves to it as freely as they can. Suggest they try not to overthink, just respond.

- The sound-maker looks out for the mover and guides them if necessary, making sure they are safe from furniture and the flailing arms of others!

- After about two minutes they swap over. They will want to talk immediately the first person opens their eyes, but try and prevent this until they have tried it the other way round – assure them they can talk afterwards. After about two minutes, stop. *Flyback*.

- What did they find out? What did it feel like? Was it easier to make the sound or to move? Did you fall into patterns of movement or sound? What sort? Did you get stuck and repeat the same sounds or movements? How did you feel if you did? This exercise tends to provoke a huge variety of responses.

Tip: When explaining this exercise, it is usually better to show them what you mean rather than explain. It's quicker and shows them you are prepared to take a risk and do it yourself. They are entertained and many are emboldened to take the risk.

Soundtracks (*Development*)

If that exercise goes well for your group you might consider the following, either straight afterwards or later:

- Get half the group to stand together like a band (Group One).

- Ask the other half to each find a space where they have plenty of room and are not too close to anyone else (Group Two).

- Ask Group One to make a soundtrack for Group Two.

- You should stay in the sound group and facilitate the sounds. Suggest that if they hear a sound they like, they might like to imitate it or work with it, so that sometimes the whole sound group will be doing something similar until someone chooses to break out and away. This creates a more flowing soundtrack, rather than a soundtrack that is constantly anarchic. Conduct and create an ending that goes to silence after about five minutes.

- Swap the groups. When both groups have tried it, sit and discuss. How did it feel? What did they find out?

Two Qualities

Ask them each to stand in their own space. Tell them we are going to look at two qualities of movement, as described by Michael Chekhov, which are going to help them be more flexible with their voices, and give their voices quality and feeling just like the coloured voices did. One is *floating* and the other is *moulding*.

Floating

- Invite them to imagine they are weeds in a small stream, constantly being moved by the water. Ask each person to feel this in her whole body. Should she lose the feeling or if a small mischievous voice inside her says, 'What are we doing this for? It's stupid!', then just ask her to gently bring her attention back to the water and allow her whole body to be affected and let floating movements happen.

- Ask the whole group, without losing concentration, to open their eyes and keep the movement going. Ask them to be aware of anywhere in the body that is not affected and put their attention there and let out a sigh. Keep going.

- Now ask them to make a sound as they float, then later, a line: 'I don't know what you are talking about.' All being well you will find their voices have a very strong floating quality. If they don't, ask them to make the feeling of floating stronger. This should put the floating quality into their voices.

- Next, ask them to stand still but keep that floating feeling inside them. You say: '1-2-3, Go!', and they all give a floating line: 'I don't know what you are talking about.' It sounds light, floating and loving.

- When you have let this go on for about half a minute, ask them to stand still, breathe in and then shake out the body.

Moulding

- Invite them to imagine they are trying to move their arms and upper bodies through thick clay or mud. Ask them to sink their knees so they feel that the effort is also affecting their legs. Remind them to breathe and feel this through the whole body. Any time the attention is lost, bring the attention back to moving through clay.

- Invite them, without losing concentration, to open their eyes and keep the movement going.

- Now ask the group to add a sound (these sounds are usually deep and full of effort), then to add a line: 'I don't know what you are talking about.'

- Ask them to stand still but keep that feeling of moulding inside them. You say, '1-2-3, Go!' and they all give the line: 'I don't know what you are talking about.' It sounds dark and full of tragedy.

- Again, after about half a minute, ask them to stand still, breathe in and then shake out the body.

- Try singing 'Happy Birthday' or a short song they all know, floating and then moulding. Give them time to engage with the imagination first, then get it into the body and then sing, keeping moving as they sing. Let them hear the difference.

Be clear that it is not about making vague 'floaty' movements. They must really try to imagine they are floating and then the voice will really be affected and they will not have to fake it. Ask them what this felt like and what they found out.

• Explain to the group about how using these movement qualities can affect the mood and feeling of how they speak in a similar way to the *Blue Voice, Green Voice* exercise they did earlier. Explain how this can be useful for playing characters who are not like us.

Part Six: An Atmospheric Piece of Text

For the final piece of this session I would like to suggest the opening voice of *Under Milk Wood* by Dylan Thomas. Use what is best for your group but what I think you need is something atmospheric with great language and imagery, and this fits the bill very well.

FIRST VOICE (*very softly*).

To begin at the beginning:

It is spring, moonless night in the small town, starless and bible-black, the cobblestreets silent and the hunched, courters' and rabbits' wood limping invisible down to the sloeblack, slow, black, crowblack, fishingboat-bobbing sea. The houses are blind as moles (though moles see fine tonight in the snouting, velvet dingles) or blind as Captain Cat there in the muffled middle by the pump and the town clock, the shops in mourning, the Welfare Hall in widows' weeds. And all the people of the lulled and dumbfound town are sleeping now.

Hush, the babies are sleeping, the farmers, the fishers, the tradesmen and pensioners, cobbler, schoolteacher, postman and publican, the undertaker and the fancy woman, drunkard, dressmaker, preacher, policeman, the webfoot cocklewomen and the tidy wives. Young girls lie bedded soft or glide in their dreams, with rings and trousseaux, bridesmaided by glow-worms down the aisles of the organplaying wood. The boys are dreaming wicked or of the bucking ranches of the night and the jollyrodgered sea. And the anthracite statues of the horses sleep in the fields, and the cows in the byres, and the dogs in the wetnosed yards; and the cats nap in the slant corners or lope sly, streaking and needling, on the one cloud of the roofs.

You can hear the dew falling, and the hushed town breathing. Only *your* eyes are unclosed to see the black and folded town fast, and slow, asleep. And you alone can hear the invisible starfall, the darkest-before-dawn minutely dewgrazed stir of the black, dab-filled sea where the *Arethusa*, the *Curlew*, and the *Skylark*, *Zanzibar*, *Rhiannon*, the *Rover*, the *Cormorant*, and the *Star of Wales* tilt and ride.

Listen. It is night moving in the streets, the processional salt slow musical wind in Coronation Street and Cockle Row, it is the grass growing on Llareggub Hill, dewfall, starfall, the sleep of birds in Milk Wood.

Dylan Thomas, *Under Milk Wood: A Play for Voices*

You can, of course, use the same starting point as we did in the last session with 'The Listeners', but here is a different way to start engaging with the text.

• Read the first paragraph of the piece to the group and let them listen. Ask them to keep their eyes closed. Do not read flatly, but do not force too much into it either.

• After you have finished, ask them to share something of what they imagined as you were reading. Did they see colours or pictures? See if you can have a discussion about what is important when performing this piece. How should the audience feel? Are we trying to frighten them? Make them feel safe? Make them laugh? What does the language tell us? What is the atmosphere? You might suggest the quality of floating as something that might be useful.

- Now ask if there are any phrases or words they didn't understand. Support them in the pronunciation too. Don't worry about too much precision with this; you are primarily trying to get a *feel*.

- You might also draw their attention to the lists of jobs in the town of Llareggub which are in the second paragraph. Explore 'schoolteacher'. Quite quickly, get them all to make a living statue of a schoolteacher. It is often quite amusing because everyone makes similar statues. Then ask them all together to say the word 'schoolteacher' as they stand in their positions. Encourage them to exaggerate a little in both the gesture and pronunciation. Once they are doing this, ask them to drop the statue but keep the *feeling* the statue gave them and say the word *as if* they were still making the statue. This will sound a bit exaggerated, which is completely fine.

- Do the same procedure with 'postman' and 'preacher'. This helps to give several layers to the speaking of each word and is something we are going to look at further in the next session. It prevents reading the lists in a monotone and highlights that we all have feelings and impressions of the people who do these jobs in our own world. Then ask them to *veil* or *cover* or *turn down* the way they say the words, but keep the feeling of the differences they found turned up inside. The result can be quite profound and advanced, but it works simply enough, connecting the voice, imagination, body and feelings together.

Showing the Work

- Split them into groups of four or five. Give each group about ten to twelve lines of *Under Milk Wood* to work on. Encourage them to split the text up however they like, and work with atmosphere and the sound of the words. Be much more conscious of the words and atmosphere rather than any 'staging' they might do. Give them a maximum of ten minutes. Be available to help.

- Have them show their work to the rest of the group. Compare them, especially if they have different atmospheres and tempi.

- Ask the group what they thought worked well in each piece. Suggest one area of improvement and try it out if you have time.

Tip: Making the atmosphere stronger might be something that would help improve the pieces. Whenever you have to ask them to do that, you need to suggest that they 'turn it up', as it is an idea they can easily connect to. When using imaginative spurs like atmosphere, always give them time to get into it.

Part Seven: Ending the Session

- I would suggest finishing with either *The Golden Hoop* (page 59) or a *Song Circle* (page 57), or you might try an easy singing round like 'Rose, Rose', or 'Ah, Poor Bird'. We will use these rounds for exercises later, so you might want to familiarise your group with one of them here. You may know them already, or you may wish to substitute something else. The tunes are easily available online.

    'Ah, poor bird
    Wing thy flight
    Far above the sorrow
    Of this dark night.'

    '"Rose, Rose, Rose, Rose
    Shall I ever see thee wed?"
    "Aye, marry that thou wilt
    When thou art dead."'

- Let me define a 'round'. Group One begins to sing and continues singing. At the end of line one, Group Two starts to sing and continues singing. If you choose to use rounds then split the group first into two to gain confidence and sing, then into four groups and sing again. Each group starts after the other has sung the first line.

- You can then have them walk around the room, away from their groups, still singing in the round. Bring them back into the circle.

- Conduct them to go quieter and quieter as if they are walking off into the darkness. Invite them to listen to the silence and close their eyes. Then open them.

- Applause. End the session.

Tip: It is good to collect easy and simple songs (especially if they are in a different language), whether rounds or not. Once, when involved in a European youth theatre encounter, I was working with a group of young people from all over Europe. Every day, one of the group taught the rest of the group a song in their language. One good thing about using a foreign language is that the sounds are made so differently. When the member is teaching a song in a different language, ask them to go very slowly, but really get the group to listen and then try it out. Though we learn like this as babies, once we get to school this is not the way we tend to pick things up. In my opinion, it is a much more holistic way to learn. It is important only to tell them what it *means* when they have learned it.

This session has focused primarily on *imaginative* exercises to free the voice. However, the floor work and technical exercises are important too if the members of your group are to get a solid grounding in voice. It depends what you as the teacher/facilitator are aiming for.

We have now completed the two core sessions, one based primarily on the technical processes of voice, and one which follows a more imaginative route. Both approaches are important if you can manage them. If you want to commit a serious block of time to working on voice with your group, you might repeat the exercises in the two sessions for quite some time before moving on.

Part 2

The Themed Sessions

Each of these themed sessions begins with a reflection on its themes and possible goals, followed by the workshop plan. Each plan is for a workshop of seventy-five minutes or so, and includes a short warm-up. I would suggest that should you have the time, or feel the group might be responsive, that you incorporate *some* floor work. I am going to take for granted that you have already used, or at least read, the core sessions, as you might need to refer back to them. The only times I have extended the workshop, or it appears as if I have, is to incorporate an exercise on the workshop theme that I know might be suitable for a different type of group.

The middle section of the workshop plan uses awareness exercises on the subject of the workshop: be it projection, imagination, playing 'real' characters, emphasis, poetry or rhythm. They are mostly fun, but it is useful to remind people occasionally *why* we are doing them. People understandably get carried away with the idea that they have permission to play. Whilst we should not undermine that, I do believe we should occasionally remind them to check in with what they are learning. As you have read, I always feel it is better to ask, 'What did that feel like?' or 'What did you find out?'

The third section of each workshop focuses on either devised or improvised text, or a short piece of drama. Sometimes this is done in groups and is 'shown' to everyone.

The workshops always end with the *Song Circle*, a singing round of your choice or *The Golden Hoop*.

The Sessions

Themed Session 1: Wake the Word takes us further into the realm of language, to truly awaken the power of sound and words. Starting on individual words, the students explore the word through sound, feeling and movement, before working on a piece of choral text. Much of the focus is on using the body to assist the students in finding the emotional content of the word or phrase.

Themed Session 2: Can You Hear What I'm Saying? revisits some of the work done in the core sessions (especially breathing) though it focuses fundamentally on *projection*, which is not only about the technical aspects of breath and diction, but also about the wider concept of projecting yourself by radiating energy. We also deal with laughing, crying, whispering, and what to do when someone tells you to improve your diction.

Themed Session 3: I've Got Rhythm looks at music, rhythm and sound in more depth, both in sound and through the body. We then go on to look at a short piece of poetic drama and a poem. We use music and rhythm as a tool to liberate spoken text through chanting and song, and work on tempo – particularly how just speaking slowly or quickly affects the feeling of an exchange. This session also explores ways to develop pitching the voice and developing range.

Themed Session 4: Speaking in Public looks at a speech with conviction, and through working with it, at emphasis; when to breathe and pitch the speech. We also look a little at sight-reading. This session is not only useful for drama but also particularly for public speaking.

Themed Session 5: Getting Real explores realistic drama and the demands of the naturalistic text. Though everyday drama appears to be more suited to young people, it paradoxically presents all kinds of problems vocally. By working on certain exercises which focus more on stress, emotion, listening and situation rather than necessarily the poetic taste of the words, we explore everyday drama, and the particular problems of making it look like you are having an intimate chat and still be heard in a four-hundred-seat auditorium.

Themed Session 6: Hark! A Session on Shakespeare is exactly what it sounds like – a session about working on Shakespeare! Where do you start? How do you make bridges across the centuries and get over any bad experiences the young person might have had studying Shakespeare in school? This session looks at the function of poetic language in Shakespeare's work, helping the group to find the emotional content of the images through the body as well as the voice, and how to use those images and atmospheres to illuminate the characters and situations. The play explored is *Macbeth*.

Themed Session 7: Your Own Voice looks at means of using sound and voice to develop pieces for ensemble work and devising; it includes the group writing their own material. The session looks at approaches using vocal repetition/singing/ rhythm and different tonal work to create moods and scenes. It also introduces choral work. This session goes back to some of the more experimental ways of using sound and text that we have explored earlier in various parts of this book, developing further. It encourages the young people to play with their voices in ways they may not have thought possible and to use them to express their own ideas.

Themed Session 1
Wake the Word

'The hidden gesture… is the true driving force of the spoken word.'

Michael Chekhov

I have already talked about the way images and social media have affected the magic of language, but in a play we cannot get away from the fact that, whilst the words are not the key to everything (except in Shakespeare and image-strong text), they are *always* signposts of character and story.

Often, when young people encounter a script, no matter how free their voices might have become in exercises, it is as if the blinds go down when they speak from the page. Suddenly they can become tense and fearful, their voices thin and inexpressive. This is both an imaginative and a technical issue, and if we do not explore both aspects with our groups then their progress might be limited. It is up to us to help them make that leap into language and have them respond to energy, sounds, imagination, thoughts and ideas. We need to make them feel comfortable with the idea that language is the vehicle for the breath and their thoughts and feelings.

Speech is very direct, emotional and immediate. *Wake the Word* takes us further into the realm of language so it becomes a real and palpable thing for the young person; something she can taste and experience.

Warm-up

More than any other of the themed sessions, this one would bene-fit hugely from a longer warm-up. You can play with any of the exercises we have done, but here is a nuts-and-bolts warm-up which covers a lot of bases in about twelve to fifteen minutes! Most of the exercises below are described in Core Session 1 (pages 27 to 60).

- *Letting It Go.*

- *Beach Ball.* Pay a lot of attention to 'breathing down' especially if you are not intending to do any floor work.

- Ask them to put themselves in the *Qigong* standing position and put their hands on their tummies. See if they can breathe in through the nose and out through the mouth, and imagine the breath is going right down inside them into their bellies.

- *Easy Stretch.*

- *Puppet.*

- *Head Rolls.*

- *Shoulder Chugs and Rolls.*

- *Hand Throw.*

- *Chest and Waist Isolations.*

- *Balancing Act.*

- Finally, ask them to stretch to the ceiling and on a clap of your hands, they drop from the waist. Do this three times and quite vigorously. Have them let out a sound as they fall.

- *Hey Hey Hee Hee Hah Hah.*

- Go through an energetic diction regime (Core Session 1, page 48). Use the *Consonant Characters* exercise (Core Session 2, page 67) if you have the time.

- Ask them to stand and close their eyes, try and get a sense of breathing down, back straight, feel parallel, knees bent. Give at least thirty seconds of silence for this. Ask them to open their eyes, and share their energy with others. Ask them to notice if they feel differently from the start of the session.

• Shake out.

Tip: A word about 'shaking out'. It's important. A shaking-out is a vigorous shaking of the body along with a sound. It's fun. The reason is to get rid of the residual feeling and tension you might find still in your body when you finish moulding, floating, etc. All theatre work can set off difficult feelings. 'Shaking out' lets the young person know her feelings are in *her* control.

Exercises

Hard and Soft Sounds

This is a good muscular exercise and a way of giving permission for expressive speech. Often when asked for a word beginning with a strong consonant, an example of a swear word is given. I think it is useful to point out that swearing is one of the few times we really use our voices expressively.

• Get the group to stand in a close circle. Ask them to watch you.

• Whisper the sound '*puh*' and keep repeating the sound.

• As you continue repeating the consonant give it a louder and stronger plosive sound. '*PUH.*'

• When it reaches a crescendo, bring it back down to a soft whisper.

• Now get the whole group to do this with you. Breathing is free (i.e. breathe before you get out of breath).

• After a couple of tries at this – and really get them to exaggerate the strong '*PUH*' – ask them to stop.

• Ask them to give a word that begins with a soft '*puh*': words like 'petal', 'puppy', 'puff' are good. Now ask for a word that begins with a strong '*PUH*': 'push', 'pull', 'power', for instance. Pick one of each, let's say, 'petal' and 'power'.

Now ask them to find a word which might have a neutral sound. That's a bit harder. 'Person', 'poppy', 'place' are good. Now ask them, all together, to say one of each soft, neutral and strong, so: 'petal', 'person', 'power'.

- Ask them to note the difference between the soft and the strong sound and what they have to do with the muscles around their lips.

- Try with a '*buh*'. Follow the same procedure (soft, strong and neutral words)... 'Baby', 'bank' and 'bang' work well.

Tip: How you *feel* about the word and the context are going to influence how you say it, but we are exploring the power of the word right now on its own. You might like to point that out.

Word Imaging

This is a simple imaginative exercise to connect words and images.

- Ask the group to sit in a circle with enough room so that you can move behind them.

- Tell them they are going to close their eyes, and you are going to say a word, let's say, 'warm'. As you walk behind the person, you touch her lightly on the shoulder and she says the word. So each person will speak the word into the circle one by one. Encourage them to be adventurous with the language. When you have done a round of the circle, try another word, let's say 'forest'. Then 'mother', 'father', 'blue', 'forest', 'gold', 'storm', 'bubble', 'joy'. Use words that are not only sensual, evocative and alliterative, but also emotional words too.

- Ask them what they found out. As they said the word or as they heard you say it, did they see pictures? Did it affect the way they said it? Sometimes an interesting discussion develops around what happens when you hear a word; that a person might put the word into a situation, see a picture, or get a feeling from the sounds. What they notice primarily is that everyone responds to each word differently, on many different levels.

Dance My Name

This is another great exercise which is fun and gets them to explore each other's name, both for sound, meaning and feeling. Ask them to be in a circle for this one.

- Ask the group each to consider a word that they maybe take for granted, that is programmed into them and they no doubt have feelings about: their name.

- Tell them they are going to make a little movement sequence of their name, maybe a movement for each syllable. Let's say the person's name is Caroline. She could perhaps make one big opening movement as if she was going to sing a carol, then draw her finger across the space... *making a line.* Hence 'Carol-line'. Caroline may respond differently to her name and focus on the sound of it, hugging herself as if she was cold and saying 'C-c-c-caroline'. On the syllable 'line' she may make a pointing motion out to the horizon. On the other hand, Caroline may loathe her name and call herself 'Carrie'. If she doesn't use the word 'Carrie', she may express her feelings about the name Caroline in some kind of snobbish pose because that is the way she experiences it. It's all fine as long as she commits to it. Each person has to make a short movement sequence and speak their name with the movement. They have three minutes (or so) to prepare it, working alone. Ask them not to think too much.

- Other tips are to be brave, especially with the sounds. That means they have to practise the sounds with the movements. Another thing that is important is that they don't just make weak, aimless movements. If you have done *Throwing the Ball* with them, remind them of how they really finish that movement of throwing the ball. Tell them also to keep it simple and avoid pirouettes or turns. Ask aspiring ballet stars and hip-hop dancers to be generous to the less able in the group as everyone is going to copy them.

- When they have the dance of their name ready, they come back to the circle. If someone is having problems, go easy on them.

- If you have time, ask each person to perform their name with the movement in front of everyone (x3). Keep things light, especially if the group is newer. This exercise is fun but can be difficult for some, so try and intuit what they are trying to do when they show their dance and maybe get them to make the movement bigger. Above all, try and persuade them to match up the sounds *with* the movement. Make sure that each sequence finishes and remains the same each of the three times through, because the whole group is going to follow it. Ask them to show what they have prepared, going round the whole group if you can.

- Now the game moves on. Let's say you ask Caroline to start. She does her sequence over and over again and the whole group copies her, not just the movement, but the way she speaks, and what they feel is underneath what she is saying. She is leading the group. When everyone has got it, someone else starts *their* name dance, and everyone slowly changes to the new leader's movements, sounds and feelings, and so on, different people leading, through as many of the group as you can.

- Ask them to notice if the energy 'stutters' between one name and the other, and try and not let that happen but make the transition smoothly.

- If you are also doing this exercise with the group, which would be good, perform your own name dance when you feel you want the process to stop and bring it down gently.

- The amazing by-product of this exercise is what it tells you about the individuals without them realising – and is a dynamic way to remember their names.

Verbing the Body (1)

This exercise is based on Chekhov's Psychological Gesture. Some people who find it hard to work with imagination may find this more useful for them, as it is a much more earthy link between voice and body.

- Ask everyone to stand in their own space. An expression I heard used was 'to stand alone, together'.

- Suggest a verb; an action that they can do strongly with the body, like 'punch'.

- Invite them to perform the action without speaking. Make sure the movement is vigorous and done while engaging the whole body. If the movement is small and without impulse, nothing will happen and they will feel foolish. Remind them of how invigorated they were by the previous exercise.

- Invite them to breathe in through the nose and out through the mouth and let out a sound as they punch. You will suddenly feel like you are in a martial-arts school. Let them continue with this for a couple of minutes.

- Now get them to say 'punch' on the out-breath as they punch with the body.

- Ask them to say 'punch' as if they were punching with their bodies, but to stay absolutely still. You will note how much more powerful the word sounds.

- Ask them what the action did to the way they said the word.

- Try a few more: 'squeeze', 'open', 'wash', 'tear', 'embrace'.

- Shake out.

Verbing the Body (2)

If you have explored the qualities of floating and moulding (Core Session 2, page 73) and you have time, you might revisit them.

- Once you have the group moulding in their bodies moving around the room, encourage them to make sounds. They may be reluctant, so you might have to say '1-2-3, Go!' It is important to remember to make sound first because it is easier to connect sound in the body, rather than words. A good way to ensure this is going to happen is to get them to breathe out through the mouth.

- Now on the back of the sound, using the same impulse and tone, have them say, 'Clear the air! clean the sky! wash the wind!' Still moulding and moving, encourage them to speak the line in the way the movement is suggesting to them, employing the sensations it is offering to them; to connect voice and body. The voice will sound tragic and intense. Then ask them to stop moving and try to keep the sensation the moulding gave them and say the line again in the same way.

- Go through the same process as above with floating. Add the line. It will sound quite different, compliant and dreamy.

- Having got the group to explore the two qualities again, imaginatively and physically, you might explore flaming or burning. Ask them to imagine that their whole body is full of flame and that they can shoot flames from their fingers and send it from their mouths, like a superhero. Really encourage them to use their bodies, and to make sounds.

- Go through the same procedure we followed with moulding and floating. Once they are fully engaged in the flaming movement, encourage them to speak in the way the movement is suggesting to them, the sensations it is offering to them. Ask them to stop moving, then keep the sensation the flaming gave them and say the line again in the same way.

Application to Text

I have used this text for twenty years. It is a chorus of the poor women (or people) of Canterbury from T.S. Eliot's *Murder in the Cathedral.* It is very dramatic and poetic yet direct, and the language is not too difficult.

If you want to find your own piece, look for something really good, poetic and dramatic. I would recommend some of the choruses in Liz Lochhead's *Thebans*, a modern retelling of Oedipus and his clan.

Here is the Eliot extract. I have split the text into three sections, which will be useful later. The Chorus bemoans the brutal killing of the Archbishop of Canterbury, Thomas á Becket:

> (*While the knights kill Thomas A Becket, we hear the Chorus.*)

1. Clear the air! clean the sky! wash the wind! take stone from stone and wash them!
   The land is foul, the water is foul, our beasts and ourselves defiled with blood.
   A rain of blood has blinded my eyes. Where is England? where is Kent? where is Canterbury?

O far far far far in the past; and I wander in a land of barren boughs: if I break them, they bleed; I wander in a land of dry stones: if I touch them, they bleed.
How how can I ever return, to the soft quiet seasons?
Night stay with us, stop sun, hold season, let the day not come, let the spring not come.
Can I look again at the day and its common things, and see them all smeared with blood, through a curtain of falling blood?

2. We did not wish anything to happen.
We understood the private catastrophe,
The personal loss, the general misery,
Living and partly living;
The terror by night that ends in daily action,
The terror by day that ends in sleep;
But the talk in the market-place, the hand on the broom,
The night-time heaping of the ashes,
The fuel laid on the fire at daybreak,
These acts marked a limit to our suffering.
Every horror had its definition,
Every sorrow had a kind of end:
In life there is not time to grieve long.

3. But this, this is out of life, this is out of time,
An instant eternity of evil and wrong.
We are soiled by a filth that we cannot clean,
United to supernatural vermin,
It is not we alone, it is not the house, it is not the city that is defiled,
But the world that is wholly foul.
Clear the air! clean the sky! wash the wind! take the stone from the stone, take the skin from the arm, take the muscle from the bone and wash them. Wash the stone, wash the bone, wash the brain, wash the soul, wash them wash them!

• Read aloud in a circle first, each person taking a line. It will most likely sound flat, which if you have been following this workshop plan will be disappointing because they will probably have been quite expressive in the exercises. When you have finished reading, you might ask them to notice how exciting some of their earlier work has been but how the excitement can disappear when we use text. Explain words or phrases as necessary.

- Ask them what the atmosphere of the piece is. This can be a feeling, a mood, or a colour, anything. They might choose: 'darkness', 'danger', 'despair', 'being at the bottom of a well', 'in prison', 'a vast desert', 'drowning in the ocean'. All would provoke a different timbre or feel to the text. Let them choose one.

- Explain that we are going to work on the piece all together so to please make sure, if they are sitting on the floor, that they are not too relaxed and that they can breathe properly. Ask them to kneel or sit cross-legged, keeping their backs straight if at all possible.

- Tell them they are going to read the piece as a chorus from beginning to end, but a person must only read when she commits to what she is saying, when she really *wants to speak*. A good way to illustrate this is with one of the many questions in the text. Half-hearted reading of a question is not okay.

- So, someone will start and read the first line (you might have to wait a few moments for this), then someone else may read the next two, or just a portion of a line or just a word, and so on, right through to the end.

- Tell them they need to really work *with* the group. If three people start to read a line at the same time, then someone might drop back or choose to read *with* another and work with them. There will be big pauses but do not worry. The pauses will be filled with the atmosphere the group has suggested. Remind them of what that atmosphere was before you start.

- They may sometimes join in only on one word if they like. 'The land is foul' is often used with several people saying the word 'foul', because people instinctively understand that because a word is repeated, it is powerful to emphasise it. This will just happen. It's very free.

- Go through the exercise once. You can read as well, though try not to lead unless the energy is flagging. Be very judicious as to your involvement. Often when you get to the end of this first reading people are shouting.

- Review the experience. Often it will be very successful and you might want to ask questions: 'How did it feel?' 'What bits sounded good?' 'Did you notice when people were involved in what they were saying?' 'Did what other people were doing and how they were speaking affect you and the way you spoke yourself?'

- Now look again at the text. The piece is in three distinct sections like a piece of music, which I have numbered. Eliot was very influenced by music and his work has great form. You might ask them where they feel the changes are. The changes in section denote a change in mood. The movement from the second to the third seems to grow gradually. Ask them what is the mood of each section and to focus on a quality or feeling. They might say: 'despair', 'desperation', 'neediness', for the first section. For the second they might say: 'panic', 'control', 'pushing down your fear'. For the third: 'despair', 'anger', 'rage', 'vengeance'. It is interesting to note that section one and section three need not necessarily be the same.

- Split them into small groups and get them to work on one of these three sections, with these moods and atmospheres in mind, for fifteen minutes or so.

- Whatever they choose for a mood, you might ask them to imagine it and breathe it in. Be aware they need to keep it simple and really *go* for something. They can split the text up between them however they like.

- Get them to show these pieces to the rest of the group. Note if they really transmit the mood they suggested. If you have time in the feedback you might ask them to try various different things. Try getting them to breathe in the mood. Maybe you could try using qualities instead: floating for the first section, a moulding movement for the second section, a burning for the third. With success this is all showing them how they can use their body to find the feeling and thrust of a piece of text and apply, to some extent, the tools you are inviting them to explore.

- Finally run one piece after another as one piece of text.

- Feedback.

Ending the Session

- I think it would be helpful if you all did a *Flyback* to review the areas you had looked at, based on 'What have you found out in this session?'

- I personally feel a *Song Circle* is a very good ending for this class (Core Session 1, page 57). I might choose a line from *A Midsummer Night's Dream*: 'Give me your hands if we be friends' as the base line; something light and positive to counteract the intensity of the text we have been using.

- But *The Golden Hoop* is good too.

Themed Session 2
Can You Hear What I'm Saying?

'Sing out, Louise!'

from Gypsy *by Arthur Laurents & Stephen Sondheim*

When a facilitator says, 'Speak louder!' (and I shame to say I did it myself in the early days) it should only be as an absolute last resort. It's an order and the young actor may be confused by it, which will make her less likely to respond well.

Remember, voice work comes from a *feeling of ease*. She might feel embarrassed, or feel she is being accused of laziness. In addition, the order can often lead to unhelpful intellectual questioning which leads to stress: 'Why am I so quiet?' 'What am I doing wrong?' 'How can I fix it?' 'Why am I being embarrassed in front of the others?' We cannot actually assume she understands she is even *aware* of her quietness, let alone how to change it, yet it is amazing how many teachers make these assumptions.

Suggesting why a person might not speak louder – usually they are not using enough breath – is much more helpful. A technical or physical approach, such as getting her to point as she speaks, or simply finding a place in the line where she might take another breath, might be effective. Or working through the imagination and asking her to try to open her arms and speak to the room, or imagine she is in a football stadium as she speaks: all this involves her in a creative experience in which she engages rather than merely following 'teacher's orders'.

At any rate, this session of roughly seventy-five minutes is concerned primarily with clarity, projection and communication. So we shall also develop Chekhov's idea of Radiating and Receiving. I have quite an intense exercise in here which should work anywhere except in a school setting where I think it might be too challenging, and you should perhaps stick to *Throwing the Ball*.

It is worth telling your group that if the audience cannot tell what you are saying, your feelings and ideas will not be expressed so well. Suggest that it sometimes takes a while to know when you are filling a space or not, but after a while you will get the hang of it.

Warm-up

Here is a short warm-up focusing particularly on a few exercises on the breath, which prepares you for the subsequent exercises and application. When I say *short*, it is actually longer than the other short warm-ups, because this is essentially a technical session. All the basic exercises are in Core Session 1 unless otherwise stated. It involves floor work if possible.

- *Letting It Go.*
- *Beach Ball.* Pay a lot of attention to 'breathing down' especially if you are not intending to do any floor work.
- *Easy Stretch.*
- *Puppet.*
- *Head Rolls.*
- *Shoulder Chugs and Rolls.*
- *Hand Throwing.* Ask what they need to get their voices to reach their partner. Plenty of breath pushed strongly through the tummy.
- Ask them to stretch to the ceiling, and drop from the waist. Do this three times and quite vigorously. Have them let out a loud, sighing sound as they fall.

- *Hey Hey Hee Hee Hah Hah.*

- Do a little floor work if you can. Use as much of the relaxation procedure as you have time for. Focus on both exercises in *More Fuel for the Body* (Core Session 1, page 44).

- Go through an energetic diction regime as described in Core Session 1. Perhaps use the *Consonant Characters* exercise (Core Session 2, page 67) if you have the time.

- Ask them to stand and close their eyes, try and get a sense of breathing down, back straight, feet parallel, knees bent. Give at least thirty seconds of silence for this. Maybe use the *Ideal Centre* exercise (Core Session 2, page 68). Ask them to open their eyes, and share their energy with others.

- Shake out.

Exercises in Breath and Projection

It might be worth asking your group what they think projection *is*. Almost everyone recognises it as 'speaking louder'. Some people might say the word 'diction'. It often promotes dark looks from group members, as they recall the word thrown at them by irritated speech and drama teachers.

For me it is simply a process where the speaker can easily fill the room with feeling and ideas through her words, and reach the audience without anyone having to strain. If you have ever been to a play where it is hard to hear someone and you feel yourself straining to listen, it makes the whole experience difficult and you can be shut out from the feeling of the play and even the plot.

From a wider perspective, as we have already noted, projection and clarity are crucial in a whole range of other social, job, school and college scenarios.

Resonance (2)

- Work from a standing position with *Resonance* (1) (Core Session 1, page 50).

- After you have done that, ask each person to put one hand to her lips and the other on her tummy. Ask them to take a breath and make a hum.

- Watching their fingers, invite them to move their hand away from their lips, stretching the arm, all the time imagining the breath is reaching their fingers. Ask them to imagine the air as a stream of gold or silver touching their fingers.

- When the hand is held out in front of them, ask them to take another breath and imagine the breath is going to the back of the room, like a golden stream from their mouths. They can slowly bring their arms down to their sides as they do this.

- Finally ask them to intone: 'If music be the food of love, play on', on one rich note.

- Ask them to repeat the line several times, taking breaths when they need to, gradually making the phrase more like real, impassioned speech, but still with sufficient resonance to fill the room. Be aware you might still have to say '1-2-3, Go!'

- Ask them what they found out.

Tip: This exercise really is helped by the power of their imaginations. It can be helpful to get them to look at their fingers as they breathe out and move their hands, to imagine and feel the breath hitting their fingers. Be aware of tension in the body, and if you think it appropriate get them to 'let go' in the shoulders.

Throwing the Ball (Development 1)

- Build up the game as described earlier (Core Session 1, page 52).

- Once everyone is throwing well with a sound, ask them to work in pairs throwing to each other, each person about eight to ten feet from the other. Check for tension, a real preparation and finish to the throwing movement and a sharing of energy.

- Give them a verbal exchange to work with. Have them say as they throw to each other:

  'Where are we going?'

  'We are going home.'

- As soon as you give them words to say, people immediately tense up. Keep them free. Ask them to treat the words as sounds and not to try to act too much.

- Introduce feeling into the words gradually.

- Shake out.

Throwing the Ball (Development 2): Radiating and Receiving

This development could be challenging and needs to be used in a relatively emotionally mature group, or one that knows each other well. You will need to demonstrate this exercise with one of the people in the group before they do it.

It is a development of *Radiating and Receiving*, using non-verbal communication. Explain there is a strong difference between how it feels to 'radiate' or 'receive', and check out that they feel that, when they 'throw' and 'catch'. We are, of course, doing this in life all the time as our energy flows backwards and forwards when we communicate. We just don't notice it.

Explain how you as the facilitator at that moment are 'radiating' your energy towards them. They, as participants, are generally 'receiving'. When they nod affirmation towards you, their energy changes inside for a second, then goes back to receiving. If they are *not* receiving but thinking about something else, they know when they are doing that too.

- First of all get the pairs to throw and catch.

- At the moment when the ball is thrown and caught, ask the pairs to freeze. Ask them to feel they are sending their energy, and receiving it from the other.

- Now ask each pair to stand facing each other about an arm's length away (this is the bit you will need to demonstrate).

- One person *imagines* they are throwing (radiating), sending their energy to the other person, whilst the other imagines they are catching (receiving). Ask them to keep the energy flowing that way.

- When the radiating person has had enough, they touch the receiving person on the arm and say 'hello', then the radiator imagines catching the ball, becoming the receiver, and vice versa. When the radiating person has had enough they say 'hello' and touch the receiving person on the arm.

- Continue to-ing and fro-ing for a couple of minutes. This is a simple but brilliant exercise. You can see though why the group needs to be relatively comfortable with one another. It is quite intimate and often in 'real life' people do not look in each other's eyes at all. Point out, when getting and giving feedback, that what they just did is the basis for all communication.

- Shake out.

Tip: Tell them when they are doing the exercise that they may find themselves giggling and that's ok. But the rule is they need to share that with their partner, get over it, and continue. I used this exercise as a basis for pauses in a play recently with a group of nineteen- to twenty-one-year-olds and they realised how much actually goes on between people in a moment of silence.

In and Out

This exercise is a fun way for people to find sensitivity about volume.

- The whole group, you included, holds hands in a circle. There is going to be continuous sound.

- When the circle is open, everyone has to make a loud *'AAAAAHHHHH!'*

- Someone brings the circle into a huddle and the sound becomes a whisper. Then someone opens it and the circle stretches wide, as the volume goes up.

- Someone brings the circle in again, and this time maybe the circle is only opened halfway so the volume is more muted.

- And so on for a couple of minutes. Obviously this is of short duration and is energised and fun. Many people probably played something like this in primary school.

- When they have got their breath back, ask them to make the circle again. Tell them to let go of their hands and, using the circle as a measure, ask them to go and stand where they think their voices generally are when they are speaking normally. How quiet are they? If they are quiet they might stand very near the centre. If they are louder they might stand more towards the outside of the circle. What do they feel are their limits of volume right now? Ask them to work on their own, to pay no attention to anyone else. Now ask them to stand in the quieter place, and with an '*ahhhh*' sound move towards their louder limit and then back again. You might have to say '1-2-3, Go!'

- Try and avoid comments from the group about the loudness or softness of other people.

- Do not discuss this in the group any further if you do not feel it appropriate, but it is useful for the individual to assess their own voice and to consider it. They often consider that their voices are louder than they think.

Walking from the Wall

Voice is challenging to teach long-term to young people because repetition and diligence is so important for the technical aspects, and this can get boring if you do not change the tempo and intensity of the task. This next exercise should, as a natural progression, come after the earlier *Resonance* exercise, but I put *Radiating and Receiving* and *In and Out* between it to maintain variety.

When I was a student I did this exercise for months at drama school and thought it completely insane until one day it clicked. If you are in a 'resonant' room it can be beautiful. I actually used a version of it in a piece by a youth theatre group in which it denoted the passing of time. You need a good length of wall to work with this. Having only a regular classroom would prove a challenge.

- Everyone stands close to the wall, facing towards it. (Be prepared for gents' toilets jokes.)

- With a hand on their tummy, each person takes a breath and makes a '*mmmah*' sound, feeling the sound bouncing back at them off the wall.

- Ask the group to take another breath and start to walk backwards, making the '*mmmah*' sound. The goal is to maintain contact with the sound between the wall and your body. Tell them to only step away as far as they can. It is important they do this in their own time. They can breathe whenever they like.

- Ask them to try not to fake it; only leave the wall as far as they can and still get a sense of the sound bouncing back at them. Once they have gone as far as they can, each person should go back to the wall and start again: making the '*mmmah*' sound quietly and then coming away.

- Let them explore this 'alone together' for about two minutes and then ask what they found out. The main thing is to ascertain that they felt the reverberation. Also ask why and when they thought they lost it, if they did. Usually the reason is they did not have enough breath.

Song: 'Ah, Poor Bird' (2)

'Ah, poor bird
Wing thy flight
Far above the sorrow
Of this dark night.'

Okay, there is the song again! You can get the tune online. The goal of this is to get the group to connect body and voice. You will need to demonstrate.

- From a standing position they gather an imaginary bird into their cupped hands on 'Ah, poor bird' (Figure 1, overleaf).

- On 'Wing thy flight', they bring the 'bird' towards the face (Figure 2, overleaf)).

- On 'Far above the sorrow' they throw their arms out as if releasing the bird to the sky (Figure 3, overleaf)).

- 'Of this dark night', they slowly watch the bird fly away and bring their hands to their heart.

1.

2.

3.

That's the basic exercise. You might like to develop this especially for those devising their own pieces if you have some good singers in the group.

- Get the group in teams to sing in a round as described earlier. Still do the movement. Sing it through a couple of times.

- Now pick one good person from each group and get them to do this in a round with the movement and allow the others to watch. It can be quite beautiful if they get it.

Tip: Some people will get this immediately. Watch out for people singing and just doing the movements rather than also imagining what they are doing. Suggest to them that this neither looks good nor does it help them to sing the song with any sense of feeling. Without picking on anyone, you might show what you mean. Try again. Ask if people get a feeling, from the movement, that they did not have before. Usually people say 'sad' or 'lonely', etc. Ask them to notice what happens for the last two lines, how they naturally bring the sound down as they close their bodies and imagine the bird has flown. Explain to people that they must imagine the bird flying away: it will get them to focus.

Tribal Stance

This is to connect the stomach movement with the volume and quality of sound.

- Have everyone take a wide stance, knees bent, hands on thighs.
- Ask them to breathe down into the belly, making the tummy big. Now get them to pull their tummy in gently: a moan should come out.
- Get them to breathe in and push harder: a louder sound.
- Breathe in and push even harder till they are making a lot of noise.
- Shake out.

Whispering

I love playing with these three: whispering, laughing, crying. It is a natural progression from the exercise before, which is about using the tummy, which is vital for projection. What's more it really plays with the idea that you are fooling the audience, which lots of young people seem to love.

- Tell them you are going to show them how to 'whisper' safely on stage. Even if the characters are whispering, they

111

still need to fill the theatre so everyone can hear. Get them to swallow and yawn first. Demonstrate this first, and explain as you go.

- Still standing in the same position as in the *Tribal Stance*, invite them to breathe down and fill the belly, then pull the tummy in strongly and whisper, 'Where are you going?'

- Remind them that the push must come from the tummy, everywhere else should be easy and relaxed.

- Try this a few times. Use a different line, perhaps from something you are working on.

Laughing

- Ask them to recall when they have watched a play and someone has had to laugh and it has sounded forced. Maybe they have had to do it themselves.

- Explain that the way to fake laughter is to use the belly. Demonstrate as you go. Breathe into the belly and pull in fast and sharp. Make a '*hah*' sound.

- Repeat and start to speed the process up, breathing and pulling the belly in over and over. It is something like a panting. It starts to sound like laughing.

- Start to act like it is funny. (Soon everyone will be laughing for real anyway.) This is a completely technical trick so stop abruptly. This is pretty amusing to watch!

- Now let everyone try.

Crying

Deep crying uses exactly the same process as *Laughing*.

- Use the belly. Demonstrate this, so you may need to practise it at home first. Breathe into the belly and pull in, but this time make the pulling-in of the belly lighter and faster, into a kind of panting.

- Start to *act* crying. You will not have to do too much. Instruct them not to push it or they will tense up.

- Now let everyone try. When you clap your hands everyone stops.

- *Flyback*. Often people will say it made them feel sad.

Dire Dreadful Diction

When young people have their diction criticised, they often 'zone out'. Here is a simple and effective way to help young actors. Let's take the line: 'Blow winds, and crack your cheeks!' from *King Lear*.

- First of all ask the group to say the line *very* slowly enunciating *every single consonantal sound* in a very exaggerated way: watch especially for 'Blow'. Make sure they really overemphasise the sounds. People are often shy to do this so ask them to 'turn it up'. The line does not have to sound like they mean it when they start. Remind them it is a technical exercise.

- Ask them to repeat the line a few times in this way. Ask them to notice where the lips and tongue go to make these sounds. How do you sound the word 'crack'?

- Now keep the line going, but start to make it sound more and more like a normal line, without the previous exaggeration, whilst at the same time keeping the sounds all in there.

- If it is appropriate, get one or two people to show the others. Make sure to give some praise with any more critical observations.

Tip: (This is my personal taste.) If you and your group are fine with it, you can sometimes get individuals to show the group as it can be incredibly useful to everyone learning. At this stage, a person cannot always hear what is a clear, focused consonant, and watching someone else achieve it may really help.

In general, getting people to work in front of the group enhances group responsibility for learning and reinforces the notion that we are all here to help each other: it is a delicate balance and ultimately it is up to you.

'Good Evening, Ladies and Gentlemen, and Welcome to the Show!'

This exercise/game needs to be done very light-heartedly, whilst at the same time encouraging the participants to offer some constructive criticism to each other. It may be the first time a person has spoken aloud in front of the group, so be sensitive. You need a large room or studio for it.

- Split them into two groups at either end of the room.

- Explain that each person in Group One is going to walk forward a few steps, one by one, take a breath and say, 'Good evening, ladies and gentlemen, and welcome to the show!' to the other half of the group.

- There is a big embarrassment factor to this exercise so maybe you might joke about that and reassure them. Tell them it is worth it because they will learn a lot about projection.

- One by one the members of Group One do this. Group Two listens: after each person speaks, ask Group Two to suggest something good about what the speaker did. Then ask whether they could hear clearly.

- Make sure there is no nasty negativity in the criticism towards the person performing. Listening and watching is useful here because they start to realise what happens when a speaker runs out of breath or has unclear diction.

- Ask them to notice whether the performing person stands still as they speak and radiates outwards towards them or whether they look at the floor or to the side. After offering an improvement, let the person try again. Just pick one thing for each person so no one feels overburdened. How much time you spend on each person depends on the size of your group and the degree to which they are comfortable with the exercise.

- Make sure that every single person has a go. Only say 'speak louder' under the direst circumstances!

Tips: I have made a few detailed suggestions here, because this is a challenging exercise for the facilitator as well. Obviously you need to help the speaker and elicit responses from the listening group. You need to be firm but sensitive. The young person is in a vulnerable position so you need to make sure your group is respectful. Here are a few things that might help:

- If the speaker is too quiet it is probably because she is not taking enough breath or her breath is getting caught through tension in the chest or throat. A good way to dispel this is to ask her to try and literally throw the sound like a ball to the audience: swinging and using her whole body. If she is embarrassed and cannot be encouraged, get everyone to try this with her. Then get her to throw the sound again on her own and this time say the line to the audience. Applaud even a small improvement.

- If the speaker starts well but the line fizzles out, it is probably because she is breathing with the ribs or/and taking shallow breaths. Suggest she takes another breath, perhaps after 'gentlemen' and note the improvement. Tell her not to rush the second breath but really take her time.

- If the voice is loud enough to reach the 'audience' but flat (like she does not really mean it), then ask her when she comes forward to throw her arms open and smile, speaking to us as she does so. Try this with everyone again if you cannot get the person to do it alone. Remember, vigorous physical movement often frees the breathing and the inhibition.

- If the voice sounds loud enough but a bit unfocused (I equate this to it sounding like the voice is leaking out of their body rather than coming out of their mouth), I suggest you use something physical to focus it. Get them to come out and point at the audience vigorously as they speak.

- If the diction is poor, ask them to enunciate more clearly. Perhaps remind them of the *Dire Dreadful Diction* exercise you have just done.

- Finally, make sure that when they walk forward they come forward confidently and with strength. Ask them to radiate their centre outwards if they have used these earlier exercises. Maybe ask them to stand and look at every single person in the audience before they breathe and then speak.

Ending the Session

I decided not to include applying the work to a text here because I think a group needs to really absorb some of this session before any kind of serious application takes place. Projection is primarily a technical issue, and technical prowess takes practice. If you are doing a production and have more time to work with projection, then repeating some of these exercises is always useful.

If they do not do some of the breathing practice at home, you are only giving them an opportunity to explore the elements we are working with rather than learning *how*. This is completely fine as long as you are clear with your teaching goals and understand that this chance to explore is what you are giving; not technical prowess. If you are looking for serious progress, you must do your best to persuade them to practise at home, then they will develop. Liken it to training for sport or learning a musical instrument.

- As usual it would be helpful if you did a *Flyback* to review the areas you have looked at just for a couple of minutes: 'What have you found out in this session?'

- A *Song Circle* is a very good ending for this class, choose a nice fun line as the base line. *The Golden Hoop* is good too.

Themed Session 3
I've Got Rhythm

'There is no rhythm in the world, without movement.'

Langston Hughes, The Book of Rhythms

This is a much lighter session than the previous one and should have a real feeling of fun to it. Some of the exercises involve singing.

I have always loved rhythm, the feel and sound of it, and how even alone it can change the sensations and feelings the words of a text can give us. I often equate plays with music, and when I am directing I am very keen to explore changes of rhythm with the actors (especially when they are students). I have included a short piece from one of my plays specifically written and performed for youth theatre to explore in this session, along with a poem. For the most part the rhythms we will be dealing with here will be strong, not the subtle rhythms of emotion and speech. The session should last around seventy-five minutes.

Warm-up

You might mention to them to consider rhythm and where they are aware of it in life. Ask where they feel rhythm is around them: a heartbeat, a clock, music, machinery, rowing, walking, running, an alarm, typing, ring tones, the sound of the sea and, of course, the breath. Explain how, even when you write your name, the sound of pen on paper has a rhythm.

Ask them if there is anyone from a city. Draw their attention to the fact that city accents and rural accents have a very different dynamic. There is a wonderful children's book by the American poet Langston Hughes called *The Book of Rhythm*, which I personally found very inspiring for this part of the work. Nearly all the following warm-up exercises we have done before in the core sessions:

- *Letting It Go.*
- *Beach Ball.*
- *Easy Stretch.*
- *Puppets.*
- *Head Rolls.*
- *Shoulder Chugs and Rolls.*
- *Hand Throw.*
- Ask them to stretch to the ceiling, and drop from the waist. Do this three times and quite vigorously. Have them let out a sound as they fall.
- *Hey Hey Hee Hee Hah Hah.* Try putting an accent on one sound, then the next to change the rhythm. '*HEY hey he he hah hah! Hey HEY he he hah hah! Hey hey HE he hah hah! Hey hey he HE hah hah! Hey hey he he HAH hah! Hey hey he he hah HAH!*' This is tricky and may take a few attempts. This is very much in the playful atmosphere of this session.
- *Consonant Characters.*
- Ask them to consider their own breath, to listen to it, breathing in through the nose out through the mouth.

Ask them to close their eyes. Now keeping the breathing steady, ask them to move the whole body in rhythm to it. Breathe in and move at the same time with the breath, breathe out and move with the breath. Get them to repeat this a few times till it is nice and flowing. Then ask them to bring it to a stop.

Song: 'Belle Mama'

This is an energising round. You can watch an online version with me leading Dublin Youth Theatre (vimeo.com/144836296). Though this version is much more upbeat, to a 4/4 beat, but you will get the basic tune online.

'Belle Mama Belle Mama eh! (Then clap or stamp, '2-3-4'.)
Belle Mama Belle Mama eh! (Then clap or stamp, '2-3-4'.)
Belle Mama Belle Ma!
Belle Mama Belle Ma!
Belle Mama Belle Mama eh!' (Then clap or stamp, '2-3-4'.)

- Once everyone has the tune, split the group into two. The second group starts after the first line plus clapping. Tell the group the clapping beats are important because, once the round is strong, you are going to add the 'percussion'.

- Once they have that then show them the percussion, which is also on the Vimeo clip. In the three beats of the three where you don't sing, you put two stamps, a clap, then one slap of the knee, another slap of the other knee, another clap, and then slap your hands on your thighs!

- When everyone has it, all start to sing the song with the percussion. Once the whole group has it, go back into a round in groups.

Depending on the singing abilities of the group this could take a few attempts to get going, but it is massively joyful and fun, especially once everyone has the percussion.

Exercises in Rhythm

Boom Chicka

This is a fun exercise that I learned initially in a great session with music and voice teacher Debra Salem, and then adapted. There are two stages to this exercise.

Stage One

- With the group in a circle, start to chant, 'BOOM chicka BOOM chicka BOOM boom BOOM.' Get the whole group to repeat it four times.

- Now ask them to go through the sequence of three 'boom chickas', but then a silent final bar of four beats. Try to stop them mouthing or counting silently. Try that a few times.

- Now invite them to invent some sounds to fit into that silent bar of their own. The sounds can be anything but must fit into the four-beat space. People challenged by this should be encouraged to be very simple; even four sounds for every down beat is fine. Tell them they should decide what to do and do the same every time.

- When everyone is ready (only allow a minute or so for them to come up with something), fill the 'empty bar'. That is, everyone does three 'boom chickas', then on the fourth bar they do their own thing. If you can get them to be physical with their own bar, this can be a lot more fun and freeing, and like all physical activity it can free the voice.

- Finally, try getting them to alternate the silent bar, so that the first time through they do three 'boom chickas' and no one says anything for four beats. On the second time, three 'boom chickas' and their own bar. Carry this on for a bit if you like.

Stage Two

- A development is to get them to walk during the three 'boom chickas', then freeze during the free bar. Tell them to move with a *feeling of ease* and with the rhythm in their bodies.

- Sometimes I tell them to look towards someone close to them or a make a strong movement like a reaching on the fourth beat. This is to further help them find the rhythm in the body. It depends on the group, of course, but the developments for an exercise like this are endless – maybe try doubling the tempo.

Breakfast Bar

This is a delightful exercise from which we can develop text and chorus (another one from Debra Salem). You split the group into three or four subgroups.

- Ask each group what they had for breakfast. Look for a mixture of funny ideas and very simple ones. Whatever they decide (or you choose) make sure there is a variety of rhythm between the different phrases. For instance, 'lemon tea and Weetabix', has a skipping rhythm and is forthright and simple. 'Yoghurt' could be repeated strongly over and over with forceful energy.

- Group One begins. Initially this is a game to get them to use their voices and get accustomed to the rhythm of speech:

'Jam on toast,
Jam on toast,
Jam on toast,
Jam on toast.'

- Then add Group Two: 'Lemon tea and Weetabix'.

- Once they have got going, add 'Yoghurt'.

- Depending on the group, once you have been doing this for three minutes or so, you can 'conduct', bringing one group higher or one lower, or adding a new group saying: 'What I had for breakfast', or getting the whole group to start with 'Jam on toast' and asking them to peel off into their own groups.

- You can add tunes for each phrase.

- Another fun variation is to get each group to make a 'routine' of simple movements for their phrase. Allow them just a minute or two to prepare this and, like *Dance My Name* in Themed Session 1 (page 91), tell them to make sure the movements are easy. There are loads of things you can add with this exercise.

- One useful reminder is to *end it properly*, either conducting it down to a whisper or a crescendo, so it really *ends*. Ask them to listen to the silence when you finish.

Tip: It would be good to *Flyback* on this exercise. Invite them to consider the actual rhythm of words and phrases. Explain and show how words like, 'computer', 'catastrophe', 'personality', can actually be beat out in rhythm. Invite them to clap the rhythm of these words. You might like to get them to clap out the rhythm of their name, or go back to the breakfast phrases and get them to clap out their rhythm. Using language helps them to use much more complex rhythms than they would otherwise have considered.

Alien Nation

Alien Nation was a forty-minute play commissioned and performed by Galway Youth Theatre in the Cúirt International Literature Festival, Galway, in 2002. It was about the growing but (at that time) fairly hidden subject of racism in Ireland. It had a number of incarnations at GYT after that, was also used in schools and performed by a number of youth theatres in Ireland and the UK. It was published by the National Association of Youth Drama Ireland's book of plays entitled *Playshare*.

The scenes are sharp and televisual, but there are songs, poetic monologues and, relevant to our session plan, choruses, built up in a similar way to the *Breakfast Bar* exercise. These choruses evolved to include singing and a lot of choreography, created mainly by the young people organically from the words. But here is one of the basic chants you can use for exploration of a text. Split the group into three. The choruses are repeated over and over.

GROUP ONE.
> You gotta *walk* like me,
> You gotta *look* like me,
> You gotta *speak* like me,
> You gotta *think* like me,
> You gotta *be* like me,
> *Be* like me,
> Be like *me*! (*2-3-4.*)

GROUP TWO.
> Walk like *me*!
> Look like *me*!
> Speak like *me*!
> Think like *me*!

GROUP THREE.
> Be like me, be like me! *Be!* (*Repeat.*)

The context is fairly self-explanatory. The chorus is ganglike, threatening and strong. Try it with different volumes and qualities. Invent other ways of working with it rhythmically. Ask each group to provide a movement sequence that everyone can learn, so groups can split and join as conducted by you.

A great thing about working with this sequence is you can do a lot with it. The idea of it is to show the group the power of spoken chorus and rhythm. Try staging it a little. Maybe have a silent group who is threatened by the speaking group.

There are other poetic and sung sessions in the play you might like to look at (see Bibliography).

The Machines of Time and Place (1)

This could be an alternative to the last exercise, or the next one in a sequence. It is a great exercise for devisers in particular.

- Ask the group to consider a place or event, let's say *an office*. We will use a slow and definite 4/4 beat so the actors have scope to play a little with the rhythm of language. You might

123

suggest it is the sound of a clock. Split the group in two so one group can watch.

- Give the instruction that one actor goes into the space to say something they would say in *an office*, and at the same time perform a repetitive action. Let's say the person picks up a phone in rhythm and says: 'Good morning, Mark speaking.' The repetitive movement and the text should be performed with the same energy every time (not as easy as it sounds). (These phrases will have to come from them. I am only suggesting some so you understand the exercise.)

- Another person steps in, standing by an imaginary water fountain: 'I went out last night. I went out last night.' Again with a repetitive movement; over and over again.

- Another joins: 'My computer's crashed! My computer's crashed! My computer's crashed!' with a repeated movement as they speak.

- So now we have three people speaking in rhythm. Add more, one by one. Try to get them to keep the rhythm and movement the same *and* with the same energy. This is very hard to begin with so do your best.

- When you have eight or so involved (about half the group), ask them to all speak louder. Then try asking them to keep the rhythm but speak sadly, joyously, with boredom. Ask them to whisper.

- Suggest they double the speed or halve it. This, of course, produces very different qualities and will be amusing for the watchers. It will probably need for them to stop and start again.

- Tell them to keep the movement going but slowly take out the dialogue. Then ask them to bring the dialogue back Then suggest they slowly take out the movement and keep the dialogue. This can produce a very interesting effect.

Tip: It is quite hard to stay in rhythm. Some people will be able to manage it. One person out of the rhythm can be interesting but for the most part try your best to keep it connected. A piece of advice you might give is that, when a group member jumps in, she gets a sense of where she starts speaking in relation to what another person is repeating. In other words, when one person says 'My computer's crashed!', the next starts with 'Hello, sir, I am afraid he's not in,' straight afterwards. This can go wrong if the other person is not on track either, but it does give the more nervous participant something to hang on to. Counting and feeling it in the body is the only really safe bet.

The Machines of Time and Place (2)

Now ask the second group to work. I would suggest you take an *event* this time: a wedding, a funeral or a party.

- Let's take a wedding. Ask them to close their eyes and imagine a wedding. What is the atmosphere of the wedding? What can they see? Smell? Then ask them to speak words into the space of what they imagine, all at once. Listen for a few that will be useful.

- *Flyback* on the imaginings. Try and hone in on atmosphere and feelings rather than personal memories. Ask what was the feel of it... 'joy', 'desperation', 'formality', 'duty', 'love', 'a sense of family' might be things you will hear.

- Now ask them to make an event machine like we did with Group One. Their ideas should have more depth than Group One. All the rules apply as before.

- Once the wedding has been established with Group Two performing their wedding machine, ask them to keep the same rhythm but emphasise the quality of 'joy'. Ask them not to think about this; just breathe it in. If they feel they are losing the sense of joy just ask them to breathe it in more as they continue with the machine.

- Now see if they can slowly change the overall quality to 'desperation', still keeping the rhythm. This is quite tricky and might require a few attempts. If you feel this is too advanced for the group, just leave it out. Try changing it finally to 'love'.

- Bring it to a close.

Tip: Do a *Flyback*. Ask them to talk about the different qualities. How did it feel? Did you want to speed up when you did 'desperation' and slow down when you felt 'love'? They might talk about how the rhythm worked against the feeling, and you might discuss how often this happens to us all the time – for instance, if you are doing something mechanical (like running) your emotions are still bubbling around in their own rhythms and directions.

Application to Text

'Tarantella': How Rhythm Can Create Atmosphere

This beautiful poem by Hilaire Belloc may be an oldie but it's a goodie. If you are choosing a different poem because you feel this is not appropriate, try and find something in which it is the *rhythm* that creates the atmosphere.

A 'tarantella' is a dance, reputedly supposed to give the dancer a feeling of being in love or being bitten by a tarantula, depending on your point of view! The rhythm of the dance is built into the poem.

What is challenging about this poem is that in recognising that the rhythm is one of the prime elements in creating the mood, the group also has to recognise that the piece requires great diction and especially competent breathing work – without a good mastery of the breath it is quite hard to achieve the kind of rhythm that you want. It teaches them that they need both, technique and imagination to perform well.

'Tarantella' by Hilaire Belloc

Do you remember an Inn,
Miranda?
Do you remember an Inn?
And the tedding and the spreading
Of the straw for a bedding,
And the fleas that tease in the High Pyrenees,
And the wine that tasted of the tar?
And the cheers and the jeers of the young muleteers
(Under the vine of the dark verandah)?
Do you remember an Inn, Miranda,
Do you remember an Inn?
And the cheers and the jeers of the young muleteeers
Who hadn't got a penny,
And who weren't paying any,
And the hammer at the doors and the Din?
And the Hip! Hop! Hap!
Of the clap
Of the hands to the twirl and the swirl
Of the girl gone chancing,
Glancing,
Dancing,
Backing and advancing,
Snapping of a clapper to the spin
Out and in –
And the Ting, Tong, Tang, of the Guitar.
Do you remember an Inn,
Miranda?
Do you remember an Inn?

Never more;
Miranda,
Never more.
Only the high peaks hoar:
And Aragon a torrent at the door.
No sound
In the walls of the Halls where falls
The tread
Of the feet of the dead to the ground
No sound:
But the boom
Of the far Waterfall like Doom.

- Ask them to read the poem round the circle, a couple of lines each. When they do this, suggest they really listen to the person who reads before them and pick up the energy they are given.

- Ask them for impressions. There are two different sections of the poem, each with a very different rhythm, atmosphere and feel.

- What is the *atmosphere* until the line 'Never more'? 'A party', 'wildness', 'dancing' might be suggested. There is also, of course, 'memory'.

- Hone in on the rhythm, as that is our task. Look especially at the text in italics and get them to clap out a simple rhythm as they read the section together.

- Ask them what they noticed. The rhythm helps to give the sense of dancing and the short lines the idea of being whirled around.

- Ask people if they would like to try to read that section on their own, if it is appropriate for your group. If you let them try, ask the others what was good about what the person did and a place for improvement. Be gentle. Give them another try, and suggest where they might breathe.

- This will all sound a little mechanical right now but don't worry. Get everyone on their feet in a circle and get them to clap and dance and stamp. Maybe ask them to imagine the scene with flamenco dancers. The idea of this is to try and get the rhythm of the words into their bodies as well. If you can really get them to let go and dance it would be great. Then add the text: 'Do you remember an Inn, Miranda? Do you remember an Inn?'

- Make the clapping stronger. If you like, get people to go into the circle and do a line as the outside people clap. Go down to line 25 ending in 'of the Guitar'.

- Now sit for a moment and read the final section from 'Never more' (line 29). Ask them where the energy goes – *down*. The beat is plodding and slow like a funeral. Ask them to get on their feet again and walk in that heavy, slow, funereal beat of the poem and say the section together. Do it with them if they need the support. Ask them how it feels different to the other part of the text. What does the new rhythm add?

- If you have time, split the group into two. Group One does the section up to 'Guitar!' Group Two does from there to the end, *and* the first three lines. Give them no more than ten minutes. Ask them to split the text between them but keep the rhythm. They can be adventurous with the rhythm and play and change it but, as you walk round, try and prevent them making it overcomplicated. Ask them to use their bodies and 'stage it' to some extent.

- Get each group to show the other.

Ending the Session

- I suggest a *Flyback*. What have they discovered about rhythm in texts and rhythms of speech? Why is rhythm important and fundamental?

- A *Song Circle* is a very good ending for this class (Core Session 1, page 57). Choose something rhythmic: 'the fleas that tease in the high Pyrenees' is a good one, or maybe a rerun of 'Belle Mama' if you want to finish on a high!

As usual, you have a bit more than seventy-five minutes of session here, were you to do every single thing I suggest, but I have tried to give you some room for manoeuvre. This is a loud class so some of the exercises will have to be in a drama-club setting.

I hope through this session you have opened up the group's eyes, bodies and voices to what rhythm can actually do and how they might use it in their drama work.

Themed Session 4
Speaking in Public

'I raise up my voice – not so that I can shout, but so that those without a voice can be heard.'

Malala Yousafzai, 2013

You might recognise the quote. It was made at the United Nations by the inspiring young woman Malala Yousafzai (now a Nobel Prize winner) after she had been shot by the Taliban because she was determined to demand an education for girls. We are going to look at Malala's speech in more depth later.

This session has particular focus on public speaking rather than acting. It is going to look at using the voice with conviction to persuade, inspire and inform an audience when you are playing a role, or if you are teaching or giving presentations. I share a lot of this work not only with students and young people but also with business students, teachers and other interest groups. Its focus is communication and it is a technical, skill-based session.

I feel it is very important that, when appropriate, we encourage a group to engage with what is going on in the wider world. This session gives us that opportunity, as well as learning about the energy and emphasis required when speaking with conviction. You might want to use the text to discuss the content in general.

You have quite a bit more than seventy-five minutes of a session here, were you to do every single thing I suggest. This session has a lot of sitting-down exercises and is working more closely with text, which will appeal to certain types of groups.

Warm-up

- *Letting It Go.*
- *Beach Ball*: pay a lot of attention to 'breathing down', especially if you are not intending to do any floor work.
- *Easy Stretch.*
- *Puppets.*
- *Head Rolls.*
- *Shoulder Chugs and Rolls.*
- *Hand Throw.* This time ask them to repeat the exercise not shouting, but still feeling they are sending the sound across the circle, as they count from one to eight.
- Ask them to stretch to the ceiling, and drop from the waist. Do this three times and quite vigorously. Have them let out a sound as they fall.
- *Hey Hey Hee Hee Hah Hah.*
- Do a little floor work if you can. Use as much of the relaxation procedure as you have time for.
- Go through an energetic diction regime as described in Core Session 1 (page 48). Remember to use the body.
- Ask them to stand and close their eyes, try and get a sense of breathing down, back straight, feel parallel, knees bent. Give at least thirty seconds of silence for this. Maybe use the *Ideal Centre* exercise (Core Session 2, page 68). Ask them to open their eyes, and share their energy with others.
- Shake out.

Exercises in Projection, Emphasis, Meaning and Tone

Opening and Closing

This Chekhov exercise is ideal for projecting and sharing your words, feelings and ideas, even though you do not speak.

- Suggest that everyone 'closes'. Each person slowly draws their body and energy in and closes the whole body like a fist. Ask them also to keep both feet on the floor so it is easy to open and close.

- Ask them to 'check in' with themselves and see how it feels when they close.

- Now ask the group to open their arms very slowly and stand up as if each person is opening like a flower; arms out and imagine the energy is filling the whole room. Ask them to say 'Hello!' Ask them to close again (x4).

Tip: Notice the participant who opens, but looks at the floor. They are not fully using the imagination. Suggest they imagine their energy is going out into the whole room.

An Exercise in Projection

I am putting this here in full, although it is also to be found earlier in this book.

- Ask each person to put one hand to her lips and the other on her tummy. Ask them to take a breath and make a hum.

- Watching their fingers, invite them to move their hand away from their lips, all the time imagining the breath is reaching their fingers. Ask them to imagine the air as a stream of gold or silver, touching their fingers.

- When the hand is held out in front of them, ask them to take another breath and imagine the breath is going to the back of the room like a golden stream from their mouths. They can slowly bring their arms down as they do this.

- Finally ask them to intone, 'I raise up my voice', on one rich note.

- Ask them to repeat the line, gradually making it more like real impassioned speech, but still with sufficient resonance to fill the room. Be aware you might still have to say '1-2-3, Go!'

High and Low

This is a fun exercise on pitch.

- Find a good middle note for your group. Get everyone to sing that note and then go, step by step, up an octave with you.

- Take a breath and come back down from that high note, note by note.

- Now tell the group you are going down. You may need a slightly higher starting note. Now lead the journey down an octave, one note at a time.

- Take a breath and come back up from that low note.

- Ask how it felt. Then tell the group that everyone is going up to the high note as we did but that you want them to imagine that that high note is the note at which they speak. Tell them to take it into their bodies and see what a high voice does to them. Suggest they imagine they are at a meeting of people with high voices.

- Go up the scale with them and let them go. Suggest they go around the room and talk to the others. Soon the place will be full of excited, superficial lightweights talking about their hair and clothes, etc.

- Try the other way, going down, with exactly the same process. Suddenly the room is full of sulky, grumpy people unwilling to say much other than grunt. (I use these examples because this is what usually happens.)

- *Flyback* with them. Ask them what they noticed. They generally realise that pitch dictated subject matter and feeling, which is interesting. They come to see that the pitch of your voice is important too and that no variety is hard to listen to.

An Exercise in Emphasis

The words we emphasise are crucial to communication. It is amazing how many people talk in a monotone or emphasise inappropriate words so that what they are saying does not really make sense – and they often don't even realise they are doing it.

- Have everyone sit in a circle.

- Tell them you are going to say: 'Yes, you will go to the ball.' The person next to you will say: 'Yes, *you* will go to the ball.' Then the next person will say: 'Yes, you *will* go to the ball.' and on and on, each person putting the emphasis on the next word in the sentence. When the final word has been emphasised, the next person along starts back at the beginning with: 'Yes, you will go to the ball.' And the process begins again.

- Ask them what they found out. Suggest to them that where an actor places the emphasis in a sentence can be crucial to communicate the emotion and meaning in the line to an audience.

- Try with: '*Who* do you think you are?' Maybe they might suggest their own line.

- What they also realise is that there is such a thing as overemphasising something, or emphasising the wrong word. 'Yes, you will go *to* the ball', for instance, starts to sound nonsensical.

Tip: Often the emphasis in a speech or performance just happens because a person has a great grasp of the character, but I guarantee that for some of the time at least, underlining the words to emphasise can be an important step in communication skills for either lecture, presentation or performance. Underlining is crucial when the language is challenging or the performer has a long speech, and it can always be changed at a later stage if it isn't quite working in performance. Intellectual sense is not everything and you may find that the emphasis will become nuanced or alter completely as you work on the part.

Dramatic Pause

- Pausing can be very powerful. You must never be afraid to pause, provided you radiate your energy. Let's try this. Go back to *Opening and Closing* (page 133). Open your arms, sending your energy out in to the space. Notice as soon as your attention wanders you start to feel uncomfortable and that's when the pause becomes silly. Many are afraid they will vanish if they stop talking and just *be*: it is not so, provided something is happening in your silence.

- Try the line: 'I need to talk about our future.' Like the emphasis game, the group stands in a circle.

- Each person is to step forward in turn. The first steps forward and waits. They are present but pausing. They then look at everyone and say: 'I need to talk about our future.'

- The next says: 'I ... need to talk about our future.'

- The next says: 'I need ... to talk about our future.'

- The next says: 'I need to ... talk about our future.' And so on round the group.

- *Flyback.* Ask whether it was hard to pause. What effect did pausing have? It draws attention to what you have just said and makes people curious as to what you are going to say next. In speeches we often pause for effect.

- Shake out.

Convince Me

Put the group into pairs and get each person to talk to the other about something they love or are enthusiastic about. The aim is to convince and persuade the listener how wonderful, helpful or interesting the subject is. Ask them to stand or sit about two to three feet apart – standing is preferable. Subjects might be: 'Why I love cats', 'Why I like a pop band' or 'How to knit a jumper', or 'Paddle in a kayak'; whatever they want. Sometimes something apparently trivial might open a door for a person, for example: 'Why I love make-up'. The topic can be anything, as long as they care and know about it, but check out it is not offensive – if they are talking about something they are enthusiastic about or love, rather than something they hate, this should be prevented. Give each person a couple of minutes to talk to the other about their subject.

- *Flyback*. What did the listeners find out? How much did the speaker look at the listener? Did the speaker talk too fast? Did the speakers share the love and enthusiasm they felt for their topic?

Walk the Walk, Talk the Talk

- Ask them to find a real impulse to walk. That can be an odd thing to instigate, so here is a way for them to find it.

- Ask them to stand in a circle and feel an impulse to walk ahead. Maybe suggest they pick a spot to walk to in the room and tell themselves: 'I really want to go there!' Ask them to feel that impulse so strongly that they actually *have* to take two steps forward.

- *Flyback*. Ask where they feel that impulse comes from in their body. People generally say the thighs, pelvis and/or the chest.

- Now ask them to find the impulse and walk around the room briskly and keep it going. Now ask them to say a few times, 'I need to talk about our future.'

- Ask them to stop and share what they noticed. Many feel the walking helps them. This is because they are moving forward towards something. It doesn't mean they have to be aggressive with the text, but it gives the text a *focus.*

- If it isn't working, get them to walk forward with an impulse and point with a finger: 'Hey you! I need to talk about our future.' Pointing is a great way to get focus in the voice.

Sight-reading

If you have people in your group who are not strong readers, you may wish to leave this exercise out. However, sight-reading can be useful in our everyday lives – during religious or social events, at school or college, when auditioning or performing, we may be called on to read an unfamiliar or completely new text – so it is a good skill to master even for the less confident participants.

- Either bring in a book for each person or get them to bring in a book they really like.

- Put them in pairs and ask them to swap books.

- Ask one person in the pair to open the first page of the book they are holding and tell them they are going to read the first ten lines to their partner. Tell them to take their time and look at the person to whom they are reading. They are not allowed to have looked at the text first.

- Then ask the second person to read her piece to the first.

- *Flyback.* Were you able to share the story? Did you have to read in different characters? How was that? Did you take your time? Were you able to look at the person you were reading to? Explain that, in order to share the text, the reader needs to be reading *at least* half a line ahead, and have it memorised before they speak it to the listener.

- Everyone does the next step at once. Get everyone to turn away from their partner, and read the next ten lines aloud, occasionally looking up, reading half a line ahead. This is quite challenging but tell the group to take their time. Give them five minutes or so. Ask them to try it a couple of times.

- Now ask them to turn back towards each other and try the same piece again, one at a time. Emphasise the reading half a line ahead and the looking occasionally at the listener in order to connect with them.

Tip: This does take practice so you might want to try a few sessions and develop it. You might want to encourage them to work on trying to read a little further ahead than half a line and observe how the punctuation helps them with clues for expression. Also, when they bring in their own reading you might want to give a few moments in which they can talk to their partners about their text. You can also explore different sorts of texts and the way to read them – a driving manual requires a different tone to a Jane Austen novel! With the appropriate group there are a lot of possibilities.

Application to Text

We now come to our practical application. If you have a large group you probably will not be able to hear everyone read, but it would certainly be good if you can get a few up to 'perform'. I am using Malala Yousafzai's speech here, but it might be fun to print out a whole number of speeches by famous people and hand them out. There is an excellent book called: *Speeches that Changed the World* (Quercus, London, 2005).

However, if the whole group uses the *same* speech, perhaps you would like to read it aloud as a group first and discuss it a little.

Now ask them to work in pairs as they are going to listen and help each other.

- Tell the group that each person is going to work on a short piece of the speech (around ten to twelve lines). They are not trying to *be* the person in any way, but must aim to be committed, passionate and clear, communicating to the audience.

- Direct them to work on three things. What are the words they need to emphasise to make the meaning clear? Suggest they mark those. Where do they need to breathe? Where might they need to pause?

- Below is Malala's wonderful speech. I have marked only the *first part* of the speech for pauses (/), emphases (_), and breathing (^). I must say again that I am not trying to *be* Malala. I am trying to put across the message of her speech. The choice of emphasis, breath and pauses are mine. I have only annotated the breath when I feel it is really important to breathe and not necessarily on a comma or a full stop.

July 12, 2013 was Malala's sixteenth birthday and on that day she gave her first public speech at the United Nations Headquarters in New York, having previously been shot by the Taliban for demanding an education for girls, and going to school.

Dear <u>brothers</u> and <u>sisters,</u> do remember <u>one</u> <u>thing</u>. / <u>Malala</u> Day is not <u>my</u> day. / <u>Today</u> is the day of <u>every</u> <u>woman</u>, ^ every <u>boy</u> and every <u>girl</u> who have raised their <u>voice</u> for their <u>rights</u>. / ^ There are <u>hundreds</u> of human-rights activists and social workers / ^ who are not only <u>speaking</u> for human rights, / ^ but who are <u>struggling</u> to <u>achieve</u> their <u>goals</u> / ^ of <u>education</u>, <u>peace</u> and <u>equality</u>. ^ <u>Thousands</u> of people have been killed by the terrorists / ^ and <u>millions</u> have been injured. <u>I</u> am just <u>one</u> of them. /

So here I <u>stand</u>… / one <u>girl</u> among <u>many</u>. ^

I speak – not for <u>myself,</u> but for <u>all</u> girls and boys. / ^

I <u>raise</u> up my <u>voice</u> – not so that <u>I</u> can shout, / ^ but so that those <u>without</u> a voice can be <u>heard</u>. ^

Those who have <u>fought</u> for their <u>rights</u>: / ^

Their right / to <u>live</u> in <u>peace</u>. ^

Their right / to be <u>treated</u> with <u>dignity</u>. ^

Their right / to <u>equality</u> of <u>opportunity</u>. ^

Their right / to be <u>educated</u>. ^

Dear Friends, on the 9th of October 2012, the Taliban shot me on the left side of my forehead. They shot my friends too. They thought that the bullets would silence us. But they failed. And then, out of that silence, came thousands of voices. The terrorists thought that they would change our aims and stop our ambitions but nothing changed in my life except this: Weakness, fear and hopelessness died. Strength, power and courage was born. I am the same Malala. My ambitions are the same. My hopes are the same. My dreams are the same.

Dear sisters and brothers, I am not against anyone. Neither am I here to speak in terms of personal revenge against the Taliban or any other terrorists group. I am here to speak up for the right of education of every child. I want education for the sons and the daughters of all the extremists especially the Taliban.

I do not even hate the Talib who shot me. Even if there is a gun in my hand and he stands in front of me. I would not shoot him. This is the compassion that I have learnt from Muhammad – the prophet of mercy, Jesus Christ and Lord Buddha. This is the legacy of change that I have inherited from Martin Luther King, Nelson Mandela and Muhammad Ali Jinnah. This is the philosophy of non-violence that I have learnt from Gandhi Jee, Bacha Khan and Mother Teresa. And this is the forgiveness that I have learnt from my mother and father. This is what my soul is telling me, be peaceful and love everyone.

Dear sisters and brothers, we realise the importance of light when we see darkness. We realise the importance of our voice when we are silenced. In the same way, when we were in Swat, the north of Pakistan, we realised the importance of pens and books when we saw the guns.

The wise saying, 'The pen is mightier than sword' was true. The extremists are afraid of books and pens. The power of education frightens them. They are afraid of women. The power of the voice of women frightens them. And that is why they killed fourteen innocent medical students in the recent attack in Quetta. And that is why they killed many female teachers and polio workers in Khyber Pukhtoon Khwa and FATA. That is why they are blasting schools every day. Because they were and they are afraid of change, afraid of the equality that we will bring into our society.

I remember that there was a boy in our school who was asked by a journalist, 'Why are the Taliban against education?' He answered very simply. By pointing to his book he said, 'A Talib doesn't know what is written inside this book.' They think that God is a tiny, little conservative being who would send girls to the hell just because of going to school. The terrorists are misusing the name of Islam and Pashtun society for their own personal benefits. Pakistan is a peace-loving democratic country. Pashtuns want education for their daughters and sons. And Islam is a religion of peace, humanity and brotherhood. Islam says that it is not only each child's right to get education, rather it is their duty and responsibility.

Honourable Secretary General, peace is necessary for education. In many parts of the world especially Pakistan and Afghanistan; terrorism, wars and conflicts stop children to go to their schools. We are really tired of these wars. Women and children are suffering in many parts of the world in many ways. In India, innocent and poor children are victims of child labour. Many schools have been destroyed in Nigeria. People in Afghanistan have been affected by the hurdles of extremism for decades. Young girls have to do domestic child labour and are forced to get married at early age. Poverty, ignorance, injustice, racism and the deprivation of basic rights are the main problems faced by both men and women.

Dear fellows, today I am focusing on women's rights and girls' education because they are suffering the most. There was a time when women social activists asked men to stand up for their rights. But, this time, we will do it by ourselves. I am not telling men to step away from speaking for women's rights rather I am focusing on women to be independent to fight for themselves.

Dear sisters and brothers, now it's time to speak up.

- Ask each person to work on a twelve-line section that appeals to them and try with their partner to decide how they would like to get the message across. If you have done the sight-reading exercise beforehand, and it is unlikely you will have time to do *both* of these exercises in seventy-five minutes, ask them this time to focus on the three elements you have suggested: emphasis, breathing and pauses.

Ending the Session

- *Flyback.* What have they discovered about emphasis, pauses and breathing in this session? Suggest a connection between technical control and being able to speak passionately.

- I would suggest a quiet ending to this session. *The Golden Hoop* is ideal, or just a moment of stillness.

Themed Session 5
Getting Real

'Realism is an effort to satisfy all the theatrical conventions necessary to the production, but to do so in a way that seems to be "normal" life.'

Wikipedia

Here, we look at realistic drama and the demands of the naturalistic text. Though everyday drama might appear to be more suited to young people – more accessible – it paradoxically presents all kinds of problems vocally.

A definition for us of 'realistic drama' might be that we are trying to convince the audience the scene we are seeing is happening in someone's kitchen or bedroom right now, that the audience are most definitely not there and there is a 'fourth wall' between us and them. There is a minimum of theatricality and the dialogue tends to be low-key and naturalistic.

Part of the problem in all but the smallest of venues is that young actors imagine they are acting in an actual kitchen or at a bus stop, wherever the scene is set. It is important to remind people they are not 'being real' in that sense, but only *appearing* to be. This desire to 'be real' often means that all the vocal and physical tension the young actor has in so-called real life is there, hindering the voice work. However, you need just as much breath as you would in any other kind of stage acting.

Furthermore, as we found out in the earlier session, projection is not just about being loud enough to be heard; it's about having a voice that is relaxed and flexible and able to communicate the feelings of the character you are playing. In addition, it's about radiating your energy out towards the audience as we do in the *Ideal Centre* exercise.

By working on certain exercises that focus more on stress, emotion, listening and situation, rather than the poetic taste of the words, we embark on a session that examines the demands of realistic drama: the particular problems of making it look like you are having an intimate chat onstage while trying to fill an auditorium. It is the nearest we get to an acting class in this book.

Realistic drama is often, though not always, about what you *don't* say to the other characters. However, this does not mean that the language is flat and empty. If we consider when we are angry and swear, the words can have a strong emotional charge. If you are telling a story, and most plays are, we still need to follow it, and go with every character on their journey.

Working with a Dialect

It might be worth discussing dialects. If the young people are using their own dialect, then what is important is that they are clear and speak with enough breath, using the consonants more strongly than they would ordinarily in their everyday speech. A free and expressive voice is what we want.

When you are doing a realistic play you need to consider what priority you place on the fact that the actor *sounds* like the character and how convincing this will be for the audience.

How much you work on a dialect is your choice. If the scenes are just good scenes and you are working on them for an exercise, I do not think you should worry about it at all. If you are moving towards a production, it might be a different matter.

Remember that understanding a sense of period, class and location all come from the way a person speaks. An option for a piece moving to production is to change the location of the play to somewhere nearer home, or you can use a play where the location is less important. Another way is to make a production as the group's 'take' on it, which gives you and the group much more leeway with regards to dialect, etc.

However, if you want to try to produce a 'realistic play', we need to note that many realistic plays are *very* location specific. For instance, if you were doing a Tennessee Williams play, the dialect and location are very much part of the fabric of the story. Plays translated from another language into English do not present this problem: the fact of the translation leaves the actor free. I think it is important to stress that doing an accent badly can be woeful and it may be better not to attempt it with your group. You need to decide.

If you are devising, of course, this issue is not relevant.

Warm-up

- *Letting It Go.*
- *Beach Ball.* Pay a lot of attention to 'breathing down' especially if you are not intending to do any floor work.
- *Easy Stretch.*
- *Puppets.*
- *Head Rolls.*
- *Shoulder Chugs and Rolls.*
- *Yoga Side-bend.*
- Ask them to stretch to the ceiling, and drop from the waist. Do this three times and quite vigorously. Have them let out a sound as they fall.
- *Hey Hey Hee Hee Hah Hah.* Using the qualities ('sadly', 'joyously', etc.).
- *Throwing the Ball.*
- *Balancing Act.*

- Go through an energetic diction regime as described in Core Session 1 (page 48). Remember to use the body.

- Ask them to stand and close their eyes, try and get a sense of breathing down, back straight, feel parallel, knees bent. Give at least thirty seconds of silence for this. Maybe use the *Ideal Centre* exercise (Core Session 2, page 68). Ask them to open their eyes, and share their energy with others.

- Shake out.

Exercises in Feeling, Situation and Projection

You might explain some of the things I discuss at the start of this session, and say that today we are going to look at acting for real as if we are really having a conversation.

There are so many elements that go into how we speak to each other: the kind of people we are, where we are, what time it is, how much we are listening to the other person, the tone we use and how we are feeling, to name but a few. In this session we are going to explore some of this, but first of all we will do a few more technical exercises to get us going.

It might be worth a timely reminder to ourselves at this moment to say that there is no point getting technical proficiency without some imaginative and emotional development, and vice versa.

You might explain that just because we are acting a scene set in someone's front room, we are not *in* a front room, that even though to all intents and purposes the actors are having an intimate scene, they still have to project their voices. If you have done the session on projection (Themed Session 2: Can You Hear What I'm Saying?) you might remind them of some of that work. I would recommend you might try one of the *Throwing the Ball* development exercises (page 105) to get people in the mood, then try this one.

Speaking Not Shouting

This exercise will need a large room.

- Split the group in half and get one half to sit and watch. You could do the exercise with the whole group at once, but it is noisy.

- Ask the working group to work in pairs, and ask them to face each other. Now they are going to have a conversation with their partner about anything – their day or their weekend, for example – and really make the connection vocally with the other person.

- Once this is established, each person in the pair is going to step backwards, still talking. They will immediately find they need more breath. They need to make the tone of the dialogue as normal as they can, as they continue talking about their everyday lives.

- Suggest they step backward till they are about ten to twelve feet apart, still talking. Ask them to keep their speech as natural as possible. Then give them the instruction to start coming back in and bring their voices gradually down.

- Swap the groups over and repeat. Then *Flyback*.

Tip: Ask them what they found out. They might complain about the noise in the room, but set that aside. Ask if it was hard to do. Ask if the breath was the issue. What happens to the voice as you step back and use more volume? Voices tend to get less varied and higher, and people shout. Emphasise it is the breath that is the key, that and the tummy muscles.

See if any pair would like to try this on their own. Let them go through the exercise. Then ask them to speak with the same power as when they were a few feet apart but to stand closer together. Ask for responses. It won't sound quite natural but you will be able to hear them. Try and get the pair to have something of the friendly feeling they had when they were chatting close together.

An Exercise in Emphasis

This game from the last session (page 135) is an important technical building block for this session, particularly if you haven't done it before. It is nice to play this game sat in a circle – and have fun with it.

Gobbledigook

- Have the whole group sitting in a circle. Find two volunteers. The rest of the group are instructed to close their eyes.

- With the group listening, the two volunteers begin a conversation in gobbledigook. Ask them to try not to just say *'blah blah blah'*, but really vary the sounds and rhythm –*'schkam far diddle ee foo'*, for instance! Let them go for a couple of minutes, then ask them to stop.

- Ask some questions of the listeners. 'Who was the stronger?' 'Why?' 'Did they know each other?' 'How well?' 'Did they like each other?' 'What qualities did the conversation have?' (i.e. was it sad/ formal/casual?)

- Only now allow the rest of the group to start putting situations on it. 'They were a mother and daughter arguing about something,' for instance. They will want to do that straight away, but try and hold back if you can.

- Repeat this with other pairs. It is surprising what we glean from the 'conversations' we hear.

- Point out the fact that the way we say something, and the tone in which we say it, tells the listener so much about the atmosphere and feeling of what is being said. Draw attention to the pauses, to the speed at which the couples speak, who speaks more than another, and the effect of that.

Tip: This is an incredibly valuable exercise to understand the value of tone, listening and really connecting with your partner. I used it a lot whilst working with the outreach programme of the Blue Teapots Theatre Company in Galway, an acclaimed theatre group for actors with learning difficulties. Freed of any intellectual requirement to connect, but on a purely emotional and vocal level, most of the participants played a version of this exercise with gusto.

Connecting the Feelings

Finally we begin to move more into acting territory. For the actor to be effective, voice, body, feelings and imagination all must be connected.

- Still sat in the circle, each person, one by one, is going to say the line 'I'm not going.' They can say it however they want. It is good to use a short and simple line like this so there is a lot the group can do with it.

- *Flyback.* What did they find out? That every person has a different take on it, sees different things, imagines different scenarios, has different feelings.

- Now change the line to 'I'm not going now.' Do the same thing again, all round the circle.

- *Flyback.* What does this tell you? Every word matters. The addition of the word 'now' implies you might have been going, but you are not any more. So we need to look carefully at what the writer has asked us to say.

- Try again. 'I'm not going now, and he can't make me.' This creates a whole different dynamic.

Application to Text

Scenebytes (1)

This exercise can take a good while. It depends on the level you want to explore it. There are many variations, and at this stage it might be useful to use these exchanges, or exchanges like them, to explore the learning.

Rather than work on a scene from a play initially, I would like to work from small, realistic scenarios. Make up your own scenebytes if you would prefer, but here are some to play with.

1. So you're here.

2. I am.

1. What do you want?

2. Nothing. Nothing at all.

1. Fine.

1. Shall we go inside?

2. No – I don't know.

1. If we don't something might happen.

2. Go on then – go on!

1. Tell me.

2. Okay – but not now.

1. Why not?

2. I'm tired.

1. You're never going to tell me.

1. I am so happy.

2. I could change that.

1. What do you mean?

2. Shut up –

1. What?

1. Goodbye.

2. Goodbye.

3. Goodbye.

2. Is this really? –

1. 'Fraid so.

3. Don't forget your shoes.

When you use this exercise, don't allow the group to make up their own words. This is a *script*, just as if they had been given a role and they have to work things out for themselves. If they make up their own scenes it becomes a different exercise.

- Split the group into pairs (and a group of three if there is one left over).

- Give each group a snippet.

- Tell them that, in their pairs, they need to first of all just read the short scene to each other, perhaps radiating and receiving if they can, to see what they get from the words and from the other person they are working with. Get them to do this a few times. This is a good approach because it stops them from thinking too much.

- Now ask each pair to produce three different versions of a scene using this text. They are basically working with circumstance and character. Give them ten minutes.

- Now ask them to show each scene they have produced.

Tip: In preparation, you will find they do a lot of talking. Try and get them to avoid it and work carefully but on their feet.

In performing them for the group, the level of improvement, suggestion and intervention is up to you. You might like to look out for a few things, such as:

- Make sure they are really listening and responding to each other, and that you can hear them. Make sure they are not speaking too softly or too fast.

- Ask them to consider whether they are responding 'for real'. Do they sound like they are really in the situation into which they have put themselves?

- If you like, you can ask the group audience to guess the situation or setting for the scene.

- *Flyback*. What did they discover? That lines and situations can have many meanings. That actors have the power to change them. That it is not just the lines that make the play but what the actors do with the lines, how they interpret them. The voice carries a lot of that interpretation.

Scenebytes (2)

In order that they can understand what it feels like to be 'real', yet still take account of the fact they are acting and have an audience who needs to hear, I would next suggest that they pick one of the situations they worked on in the exercise above, and rehearse it again.

- Ask one pair to do the scenebyte as realistically as they can, in their own voices as if there was no audience to consider. People will laugh because they will probably not be able to hear anything.

- Now watch all the pieces and discuss them. Could the audience hear? Was it believable? Did they sound like they were working together and listening to each other? What you are exploring here is how do you make a scripted scene appear 'real'?

- You might draw their attention to the breath. Explain that if they breathe from their bellies, as has been explored in several earlier sessions within this book, they can keep the body relaxed and easy whilst at the same time make the voice louder. Remind them that the voice does not just have to reach a fellow actor, but every single person in the audience.

- You might do a few exercises around the breath as the whole group tries the lines of their scenebyte very technically, breathing into the belly, and intoning them into the space, then finally keeping the projection going but speaking more normally.

- See if you can get one of the pairs to try the *Speaking Not Shouting* exercise earlier in this session. Ask them to stay as 'normal' as possible as they start to step apart. Ask them to act their little scene again but using their voices as if they were apart.

- Shake out and *Flyback!*

Application to Text

If you have time you might want to take this learning to the next stage, which is working on an actual scene from a play. Here are some tips:

- Don't give them a scene longer than a page, and ensure there is some emotional shift. Remember this is primarily a voice session, and if you pick a scene that is too long, your learning goal will deal more with acting the scene than the voice work.

- If in a school, you might like to use something they are working on in class.

- Limit their preparation time. Start by getting them to radiate and receive the text first with each other so they get a sense of it and how each other might act.

- Make them do this standing up. If they sit, they will slump and engage only their heads, and their energy will sag. Then they can start to stage the scenes a little.

- In a sense this is just an exercise in basic stagecraft – cheating out and speaking up when they face the back of the stage, etc. However, it might help to give them more of an idea of the importance of being heard.

Here are some good plays to use, all from different decades:

Pronoun by Evan Placey
Buzzing to Bits by Mark O'Rowe
City Sugar by Stephen Poliakoff

Ending the Session

- As usual, a *Song Circle*, *The Golden Hoop*, or a song-in-the-round you have found yourself is a beautiful way to finish.

Themed Session 6
Hark! A Session on Shakespeare

'When today's actor starts to experience as a whole-body process she is led to a larger and deeper experience of thought and emotion.'

Kristin Linklater

In this session you and your group are going to be working on Shakespeare. It will be an exploratory workshop in which we will use *Macbeth* for our exercises, as it is one of the most accessible of Shakespeare's plays, and is frequently used for study in schools.

Many of the exercises used in the core sessions and in Themed Session 1: Wake the Word, would be especially relevant here. Vocally, Shakespeare is very demanding, but by using the earlier exercises as a foundation, it is possible to build a bridge from the play to your young people. For schoolteachers, many of the exercises might be useful for written work too, exploring themes, story and character in a more accessible and profound way than just by talking about them. Working with emphasis and underlining the words that carry the sense (as we have done in a previous session) can be enormously beneficial. I have done a number of exciting Shakespeare productions with young people, and the energy, commitment and enthusiasm have often surmounted many of the technical issues involved.

Where do you start? How do you overcome the dull and academic approach so often found in the classroom, which may well be a legacy you have to deal with even if you are not exploring this within a school setting? I would suggest that if you have time, you show the 'performance' section of the film, *Shakespeare in Love* (1998), directed by John Madden. It takes about ten minutes and, however fanciful and idealistic it might be in some respects, it does illustrate some very important points. After watching it, I might then throw the subject open for discussion. 'In what way is the performance of the play different to how it may be performed today?' Here are a few things we might like them to have seen.

1. The theatre was open to the air, therefore there was no lighting. This meant the lighting provided no atmosphere, nor did it allow for anyone to be 'discovered' on the stage (there was no 'Lights up!' and no curtain). The characters had to come on speaking as if in the middle of a discussion to grab people's attention. This gave the plays incredible pace.

2. There was little or no scenery. This meant the language and costume had to carry all the weight of atmosphere and location, to support the story, character and psychological development. (I believe audiences were quite comfortable with that, as the film attempts to show.)

3. The audience came from *all* walks of life. This meant that the plays had to have something to appeal to every single group.

4. The audience was very near the stage. Some nobles sat *on* the stage (though this does not happen in the film). This made for a very flexible relationship with the audience, rather than a feeling of separation between performers and watchers. The audience and actors could see each other. Sometimes the audience was directly addressed, often within a scene, so they could be confidantes and co-conspirators with the characters.

Why is it important to share and explore this? I strongly believe that if a young person appreciates *why* Shakespeare's plays were written in this way, and understands the power the language had for the audience and what it had to achieve, it will go a long way towards helping them be able to play it.

'If it were done': Poetry and Prose

If you are confident as a performer yourself, you may find this exercise very useful. A common issue for young people is dealing with the poetry in the language, and so it is helpful to consider why Shakespeare and his peers wrote in such a heightened, poetic way. Some of these issues have already been explored in discussing the film, but this will develop their understanding further.

- Tell them you are going to read/act a monologue from *Macbeth*, Act One, Scene Seven. All they need to know is Macbeth is trying to decide whether to kill the King visiting his castle, and so become King himself.

- You will see two versions of the speech below; one is the original and one a modern version. Read both pieces as well as you can, obviously with the script, though it might be useful to rehearse them at home so you can make eye contact with the group. Afterwards, ask the group what the differences were between the two pieces. Only later ask which they prefer. Many will prefer the literal translation so be prepared!

1. If it could just be over; if the murder, the assassination – if we knew it was going to succeed – if we were definitely going to get away with it... Well, then I wouldn't care what happens in the afterlife! I'd jump the life to come.

   But the thing is, I know that if you do something evil, that it will come back to you. We all know this. You can't get away with a crime this big. It's almost like – well we're hurting ourselves in the end by doing it. It's like we are killing ourselves. It comes back. You can't escape it...

   There are two good reasons why I shouldn't do it. For a start he's family; we're related. And it's not only that, but I'm his host! He's a guest in my house. I should be protecting him from his enemies, not planning to kill him myself.

Besides, Duncan has been such a good king, such a noble king, that all his goodness just screams out against the murder. And the whole world will grieve, and Heaven will cry out against it, and cry out against me, the murderer... I'll be damned forever.

2. If it were done when 'tis done, then 'twere well
It were done quickly: if th' assassination
Could trammel up the consequence, and catch
With his surcease success; that but this blow
Might be the be-all and the end-all here,
But here, upon this bank and shoal of time,
We'd jump the life to come. But in these cases,
We still have judgment here; that we but teach
Bloody instructions, which, being taught, return
To plague th' inventor: this even-handed justice
Commends the ingredience of our poison'd chalice
To our own lips. He's here in double trust;
First, as I am his kinsman and his subject,
Strong both against the deed; then, as his host,
Who should against his murderer shut the door,
Not bear the knife myself. Besides, this Duncan
Hath borne his faculties so meek, hath been
So clear in his great office, that his virtues
Will plead like angels, trumpet-tongu'd, against
The deep damnation of his taking-off;
And Pity, like a naked new-born babe,
Striding the blast, or heaven's cherubins, hors'd
Upon the sightless couriers of the air,
Shall blow the horrid deed in every eye,
That tears shall drown the wind.

- *Flyback*. There are obvious things people might say. The Shakespeare is harder to understand but all-engulfing. The images are very powerful. It has a strong rhythm. The poetry makes it feel like it's about more than just one man, more universal. The realistic version is easier to understand, shorter but flatter. Some people feel the realistic version allows them to understand Macbeth better and some will not agree. What's important is that they explore the differences around how the *poetry* makes them feel and how the modern *prose* makes them feel.

It might be worth considering these differences yourself, if in teaching Shakespeare you think it is better to get the story across along with a few useful quotes for an examination. Modernising Shakespeare is not always successful and it might be worth looking at a short but excellent book by Peter Brook called *Evoking (and Forgetting) Shakespeare*, which explores the trade-offs of updating a Shakespeare play.

Warm-up

Now it is time to get them on their feet. Most of this warm-up is from Core Session 1. Try and incorporate some floor work if you have the time.

- *Letting It Go.*
- *Beach Ball.* Pay a lot of attention to 'breathing down', especially if you are not intending to do any floor work.
- Ask them in the *Qigong* position to put their hands on their tummies. See if they can breathe in through the nose, out through the mouth and imagine the breath is going right down inside them.
- *Easy Stretch.*
- *Puppets.*
- *Head Rolls.*
- *Shoulder Chugs and Rolls.*
- *Hand Throw.*
- *Chest and Waist Isolations.*
- *Balancing Act.*

- Ask them to stretch to the ceiling, and drop from the waist. Do this three times and quite vigorously. Have them let out a sound as they fall.

- *Hey Hey Hee Hee Hah Hah.*

- Go through an energetic diction regime as described in Core Session 1 (page 48). Use the *Consonant Characters* exercise of Core Session 2 (page 67) to get the sound into their bodies if you have the time.

- Get them to do some humming, focusing on the head, the bridge of the nose, the lips and the chest.

- Ask them to stand and close their eyes, try and get a sense of breathing down, back straight, feet parallel, knees bent. Give at least thirty seconds of silence for this. Ask them to open their eyes, and share their energy with others. See if they feel any different.

- *Shake Out.*

In On It: Sharing with the Audience

I devised this game to give young people the chance to explore the actor's relationship with the audience and how the Shakespearean model plays with it.

- Ask them to get into pairs.

- Tell them they need to make up a short improvisation between two people who are not necessarily telling the truth to each other. Ask them to consider times in their everyday lives when they are thinking something different to what they are actually revealing: job interviews, attempts to lie to keep out of trouble, meeting a demanding friend who is telling them some personal secret, etc.

- Each pair performs their improvisation to the group, acting both with their partners and also giving 'asides' to their 'other partner' (the audience) about what is happening onstage. In Shakespeare's plays the audience is frequently treated as a co-conspirator or friend. (To my mind, this is a much more enjoyable starting point than saying that soliloquies and/or asides are about people talking to themselves.)

• If you are going to give everyone a turn it will be quite a long exercise, but it is a great way to get them to play with the audience/actor relationship, have fun and perform! Be selective if you do not have the time.

Here is a funny idea as an example. A mum with a school-age child who is misbehaving has been asked in to see the principal.

PRINCIPAL. Ah, Mrs Harrison, come in.

MRS H (*to audience*). I've had to miss my lunch hour for this. (*To* PRINCIPAL.) Thanks a lot. What do you need to see me for?

PRINCIPAL (*to* MRS H). Mind if I have my lunch?

MRS H (*to* PRINCIPAL). Noooo. (*To audience.*) There is nothing wrong with Charlie. He's just a bit... lively. Whatever you hear in the next few minutes, she's a liar.

PRINCIPAL (*to* MRS H). Thank you. It's about Charlie.

MRS H (*to audience*). She makes me feel like I did something wrong! Guilt trip! (*To* PRINCIPAL, *sourly.*) What's he done?

PRINCIPAL (*to* MRS H). Do you know Mrs Campbell?

MRS H (*to* PRINCIPAL). Yes. (*To audience.*) Boring cow!

PRINCIPAL (*to* MRS H). She teaches maths.

MRS H (*to audience*). She bored me to death! You can see this is going to turn out badly already!

You get the idea. Encourage them to play with this idea of sharing their thoughts and looks with the audience, whilst at the same time keeping the scene going. Some of the dialogue will overlap and it will be rough, but the idea of sharing with the audience will be implanted.

Rhythm Works

Give out this short section from Act Two, Scene Two of *Macbeth*. I have suggested a whole number of approaches here which you might find useful.

LADY MACBETH.
    Alack, I am afraid they have awak'd,
    And 'tis not done. Th' attempt and not the deed
    Confounds us. Hark! I laid their daggers ready;
    He could not miss 'em. Had he not resembled
    My father as he slept, I had done't.

Enter MACBETH.

                         My husband!

MACBETH.
    I have done the deed. Didst thou not hear a noise?

LADY MACBETH.
    I heard the owl scream, and the crickets cry.
    Did not you speak?

MACBETH.
            When?

LADY MACBETH.
            Now.

MACBETH.
                As I descended?

LADY MACBETH.
    Ay.

MACBETH.
    Hark! Who lies i' the second chamber?

LADY MACBETH.
                    Donalbain.

MACBETH.
    This is a sorry sight.

Looking on his hands.

LADY MACBETH.
    A foolish thought, to say a sorry sight.

- You might explain that Shakespeare's poetry is written in a rhythm of ten beats. (You can go into this in more depth if you are going to work towards a production and explain about iambic pentameter, but that is not the real point of this exercise.) You might like to explain that some scenes and characters are written in prose and these are generally (though not always) the comic characters.

- Explain that Macbeth has just murdered the King and his wife is waiting for him downstairs. It is the dead of night. Everyone else in the castle is asleep and it's dark.

- Get them to read the script aloud. Help them out with difficult words.

- Once through the scene, ask them what the atmosphere of the scene is like. They might say 'secret', 'evil', 'dangerous', 'nervous', 'dark'.

- Use these words as a springboard. Get them to read the short scene again, either using two people in front of the whole group or get the whole group to work in pairs. Suggest they go for a quality of secrecy. Tell them to try whispering.

- Another tack is to get two of the keener actors to try reading with the quality of secrecy, whilst the rest of the group whispers and creates a dangerous atmosphere for the main actors.

- It is useful to ask them to look at the script and consider the line structure. What can the staggered lines mean? The answer, of course, is speed, urgency, danger, panic.

- Ask them to work on reading the lines fast in their pairs, or very slowly. Ask them how does going fast or slow affect the scene.

- You might ask them now to breathe in an atmosphere of darkness and to feel what that is like in their bodies, to try and hold that feeling in the body and then read the scene. When you ask them to breathe in a feeling like that, *always* make sure that you ask them to shake it out afterwards.

- You can continue with this scene and stage it a little if you so choose.

Tip: Never underestimate the power of the rest of the group to help create an atmosphere for the main actors in a scene.

Physical Phrases

This is a variation of *Verbing the Body* (page 93), inspired by a Kristin Linklater exercise in her book, *Freeing Shakespeare's Voice.*

Have each person work on their own at the same time.

- Ask each person to make a movement for the word 'tough'. Get them to repeat the movement a few times. Ask them how it feels in their bodies.

- Then ask them to say the word quietly as they make the move and then make the word louder. Ask them to keep the feeling in their bodies and then on '1-2-3, Go!' from you, say 'tough' all together. You will be surprised at the power of it.

- Now ask them to repeat the process with the word 'love', going through exactly the same process, until they have all said 'love' together.

- You can now ask them to put the two words together, separately first. Then ask them to say 'tough love' as one phrase, but keeping something of the different feel of the individual words. You might need to reintroduce the physical movements first.

- *Flyback*. Some people might notice how they could say the phrase yet still keep some colouring of each individual word. Remind them how a word or phrase has many levels and how this was understood in Shakespeare's time. You could try this again with another phrase: 'dangerous / games', 'open / house', 'mobile / phone'.

Exploring an Image (1)

This exercise leads on from the last and also develops the work in Themed Session 1: Wake the Word.

Suggest to the group that there is no value to be gained from ignoring images within a text. They can be a gateway to understanding how the character is feeling and create the right atmosphere. Unfortunately, as I discovered in a recent professional London production I saw, there are still a lot of actors and directors who speak the images as if they were to be ignored in favour of speed or for fear they might bore the audience, when in actual fact they are what gives the plays much of their depth. Let's use some of this piece from Act Three, Scene Two of *Macbeth* to explore this fact. It is an ominous and scary section: Macbeth has just set his latest murder in motion.

> Light thickens, and the crow
> Makes wing to th' rooky wood.
> Good things of day begin to droop and drowse;
> Whiles night's black agents to their preys do rouse.
> Thou marvel'st at my words: but hold thee still;
> Things bad begun make strong themselves by ill.

- Split the group into three groups of five (say). If you have a bigger group then some lines can be worked on by more than one group.

- Allot the small groups either one or two lines.

- Tell them that, as a group, they are going to find an expressive gesture for each individual word in the line. As they make each gesture, together they say the word. For instance, for 'Light', the group might open their arms and look out and up as they speak. For 'thickens' they might slowly bring their hands together, and their voices become darker... and so on.

- For 'and' (and it is essential they have a movement/statue for *all* the words, even the small ones), ask them to make a

167

gesture which emphasises the *job* of the word. 'And' is a joining or adding word, for instance.

- When each small group has a set of gestures and a way of saying the whole line together, ask them to perform it for the other groups.

Tips:

- Make sure at this point that they keep the words as separate units: i.e. it is 'Light / thickens' not 'Light thickens', in other words, they are pulling even the image apart.

- Make sure that each gesture galvanises the way they say the word and that the gesture and voice are connected. All you can do is suggest this. For some people you will get only a glimmer of initial success, but this is a powerful exercise and worth exploring.

Exploring an Image (2)

- Once they have shown their gestures and spoken their line, go round each group again. Ask them to move and speak as before, showing the others.

- Now ask them to try and speak the line exactly as before but this time without the gestures. It will still sound staccato and a bit artificial, but many of them will be exploring language in ways they never did before.

- It is always useful to suggest that doing more is always better than doing less! They might hold back from this, and other exercises, because they are nervous.

- After one group has shown without the gestures, ask them to speak the line, keeping the differences but starting to add the *sense* of the line. It will still be a little ponderous but the richness will be apparent. Go round all the groups using this procedure.

- *Flyback.* What is amazing with this exercise is revealing the power of a single word, and the colouring and emotional depth you can get into a phrase. It really lets people in to the power of spoken language.

Application to Text

There might be time to look at a scene. The first scene of Shakespeare's *Macbeth* is one of the shortest and most exciting in the canon.

Scene: a heath.

Thunder and lightning. Enter three WITCHES.

1 WITCH.
    When shall we three meet again
    In thunder, lightning, or in rain?

2 WITCH.
    When the hurlyburly's done,
    When the battle's lost and won.

3 WITCH.
    That will be ere the set of sun.

1 WITCH.
    Where the place?

2 WITCH.
                    Upon the heath.

3 WITCH.
    There to meet with Macbeth.

1 WITCH.
    I come, Graymalkin!

2 WITCH.
    Paddock calls!

3 WITCH.
    Anon!

> ALL.
>> Fair is foul, and foul is fair;
>> Hover through the fog and filthy air.
>
> *Exeunt.*

- Explain any words that people might not understand. Note the fact that the witches are waiting and asking questions, and that they are talking about a battle that hasn't even happened yet.

- Get three people to read it and have the others close their eyes.

- Afterwards ask them what the listeners saw or felt in their imaginations. Reject nothing but look for 'a sense of doom', 'one lonely dead tree', 'a large empty space', 'a need to know', 'an icy wind', and so on.

- Split the group into threes, one for each witch. If you don't have the right number, suggest they add familiars, animals, or perhaps the spirit of Macbeth into the scene. Be creative. Someone might want to create a soundtrack.

- Let's suppose imaginative responses were given, similar to the ones I suggested above. Suggest they pick one or think up another. Let's take 'a large empty space' as an example: our three actors will play the scene like it is in a large moorland space. Or maybe the emptiness is inside them. Try to link the imaginative ideas to the way they might speak the piece.

- If you don't want to focus them like that, you can allow them to be completely free in their scenarios, provided they do not spoof it. Ask them to play the scene seriously and not to send it up, which will be a great temptation. The goal of this exercise is that they find a truthful essence to the piece.

- Suggest they decide which witch has the highest status from the text (maybe there isn't one).

- Ask them to consider what a witch *is*. I would suggest that you say that Hallowe'en witches are out of bounds.

- Support, assist as much as you feel appropriate, and show and give feedback as we have discussed.

Ending the Session

- *Flyback.* You might like to consider with the group how far you have come and what they may have learned about performing Shakespeare from this session. Whilst there is a lot of material here, I would not necessarily expect a group to do it all. The session is text-based and, whilst we have only used small pieces of text, it may not suit everyone. You have to explore what is best.

- If you end with a *Song Circle* you might use as a line of text: 'When shall we three meet again?' You could use 'Rose, Rose' (page 79) as a song from the period of the play.

Themed Session 7
Your Own Voice

'What is a voice for? In order to say something! What
do you want to say? – as a person, as an actor… a
subject that you want to say something about, for
example political, personal, artistic.'

Sarah Case

The focus of many youth groups is devising pieces of theatre.
It seems more relevant, more exciting and more urgent. This
session looks at means of using sound and voice to develop
pieces for ensemble and devised work, such as creating soundscapes and soundtracks. The work is often about how you can
create powerful effects and includes more application for actual
performance. This approach to voice may appeal to some
groups, encourage them to play with their voices away from text
and help them express their own ideas.

Many of the exercises we have done already have a powerful
impact and can be developed for pieces in performance. Some
you could use might be:

*   *Soundtracks* from Core Session 2 (page 71)

*   *Walking from the Wall* from Themed Session 2: Can You
    Hear What I'm Saying? (page 108)

*   *Boom Chicka / Breakfast Bar / The Machines of Time and Place*
    from Themed Session 3: I've Got Rhythm (pages 120, 121,
    123)

- *Gobbledigook/Scenebytes* from Themed Session 5: Getting Real (pages 150 and 151)

All work well for devising and I describe some ways of developing them in this chapter.

An Introductory Exercise: Sound into Movement

- To start with, ask them to stand in a circle and close their eyes. Ask them to feel themselves in the *now*, and listen to the sounds outside. Perhaps there is traffic or birdsong. Ask them to breathe in those sounds.

- Now ask them to bring their focus closer, into the room you are working in. Can they hear a clock? The breathing of others? Someone coughing? Ask them to take one of these sounds and with their eyes closed, really listen, then use the sound as *inspiration* to make a movement. For instance, if they hear the sea outside the room they might make a flowing movement. If it is a bird they might make a fluttering light movement. If it's traffic they might make fast movements in all directions (without moving round the room though – they have their eyes closed!).

- Then ask them to add their own sounds to the movements: build the sound for about half a minute and then bring it down to silence. Ask them to open their eyes and shake out.

Tip: This simple little exercise reminds us of so much. It shows us the rhythm and quality of sound, and how it mirrors the way we speak, act and feel. It reminds us how important it is to *listen*. So much of responding to someone in words is about listening to what they say and to the energy with which they say it.

Warm-up

In addition to the warming up of the instrument, the main focus of this warm-up is to get people to respond creatively and imaginatively through the exercises.

- *Letting It Go.* Leave this out if you have done the suggested introductory listening exercise above.
- *Beach Ball.* Pay a lot of attention to 'breathing down', especially if you are not intending to do any floor work.
- *Easy Stretch.*
- *Puppets.*
- *Head Rolls.*
- *Shoulder Chugs and Rolls.*
- *Hand Throw.*
- *Chest and Waist Isolations.*
- *Balancing Act.*
- Ask them to stretch to the ceiling, and drop from the waist. Do this three times and quite vigorously. Have them let out a sound as they fall, then come up slowly.
- *Hey Hey Hee Hee Hah Hah.* Using the qualities ('sadly', 'joyously', etc.).
- *Consonant Characters.*
- Ask them to stand and close their eyes, try and get a sense of breathing down, back straight, feet parallel, knees bent. Give at least thirty seconds of silence for this. Ask them to open their eyes and share their energy with others. See if they feel any different.
- Ask them to close their eyes again and then imagine that the belly is full of a dark-blue colour, so that when they breathe out dark-blue air pours out from each person's mouth. Ask them to let their imagination lead them and on '1-2-3, Go!', ask them to see if a sound comes out and let them develop this. They may well be shy. Try and get everyone to keep the sound going and have their eyes shut for maximum ease and less embarrassment. Ask them with the blue voice to try saying: 'And so they set out to sea.'
- Ask them to shake out and then repeat the exercise imagining a blood-red colour. Let them try the line again:

banana-yellow, purple, silver. As this is a very potent exercise, which people often take literally, I would avoid green!

- *Flyback* on this exercise. People often find this exercise a bit strange as they are making sounds they are not used to. Explain how a character could have a certain colour of voice, which is very useful when you have many parts to play in a piece.

Making Sound and Listening

Leading Sounds

An oldie but a goodie.

- Ask the group to join into pairs. Ask one partner to close her eyes. That person is the 'follower'. Tell the person with open eyes they are going to lead the follower around the room, only by making a particular sound and pitch. Leader and follower must not touch.

- *Please note*: This is not like *Soundtracks*, where the sound-maker is encouraged to be as creative as possible. They need to make their range of sounds distinctive to their follower.

- Make sure the person with closed eyes knows what their partner's sound is and then let all the leaders try taking their followers round the room with their voices. People can get quite ambitious with this and even alter the quality of the sound to encourage the follower to lead cautiously or quietly, say, when the leader makes cautious or quiet sound.

Soundscapes (1)

This exercise is directly useful for creating original work.

- Ask the group to lie down on the floor with their heads fairly close together. Tell them you are going to say a word, and ask them to breathe in the word, see the pictures, smell the smells or whatever the word gives to them. 'Ocean' is a good one to start with.

- Tell them that you do not necessarily want them to make the sound of the sea, or gulls, or a ship's horn. They might decide to make a 'blue' sound.

- Once each person has established their sound for a couple of minutes you will then ask each of them to listen to other sounds as they continue to make their own. If one hears a sound she likes, she could start to make it too, so at any time there might be four or five people making the same sound whilst others continue with their own sound. Ask them to be sensitive, like an orchestra playing a piece of music, so that maybe at one point the whole group is making the same sound.

- Then ask them, in their own time, to pick up another sound they like so the whole wave starts again. Tell them that they will be in charge of this: not you. They will get a sense of the group movement of the sound.

- Try other soundscapes: 'forest' or 'wasteland', for example. Then move on to moods: 'peace', 'war', 'loneliness', 'secrecy', 'festival'. Maybe try a colour. Try not to allow them to be too literal.

- *Flyback.* This exercise can be quite profound in that people can realise they have very different responses to the words and concepts, but that by exploring and experiencing each other's sounds they can make a tapestry and find a richness in their soundscapes. It can also be a very relaxing exercise. It is very helpful at connecting the group as a creative unit.

Soundscapes (2): Application

Ask them how they think using soundscapes might be useful in a play or to help with telling a story. They can provide the mood, the environment, the atmosphere or the very thoughts of the characters, and move us into the idea of having a chorus of actors.

- Try this or make up your own scenario: one person is to make a slow journey to a door, open it and go in. The actor has to behave as if she is battling with a terrible wind.

177

- Now ask the actor to repeat the scenario, but this time ask the rest of the group to make a strong, gusting wind sound. When the actor shuts the door, the wind lessens.

- Try it again and this time ask the group to allow the wind to die just before the person opens the door. Ask the performer to respond to it before she goes in. It will seem strange and supernatural.

- Try it one more time and this time the actor has powers. Before she opens the door, she throws her arms open and shouts 'NO MORE!' and the wind stops abruptly. Then she goes in.

- Try other scenarios.

Tip: Build the exercise up slowly.

- *Flyback*. The relationship between the chorus and the solo actor is a very collaborative affair. The wind can both empower the character the actor is playing or threaten them. This sound/voice exercise has a lot to show us about the core of acting and communication.

Soundtracks (2)

This exercise, where one person provides a soundtrack for another whose eyes are closed, might be worth exploring here. I will recap the basic rules:

- Ask the group to go into pairs. (A three would work too.) One of the pair is going to close her eyes (two if it's a group of three).

- The one with eyes open is going to make a soundtrack for the other person to move to.

- The person with their eyes closed responds to the soundtrack and moves to it as freely as they can. Suggest they try not to overthink, just respond.

- The sound-maker looks out for the mover and guides them if necessary, making sure they are safe from furniture and the flailing arms of others!

- In this development, encourage the sound-maker to make sounds and dialogue for how the person might be *feeling and thinking.* The person with their eyes closed must behave as if these sounds, thoughts and sentences, are their own. A text might be: 'I wonder if she's gonna call me, after what I said to her... I didn't mean to do that. I mean, when I saw her, I just got things wrong... I made a MISTAKE! ALL RIGHT I MADE A MISTAKE! I am in so much trouble.'

- After about two minutes, swap over roles.

Application

The previous exercise is a lead-in to a more complicated chorus exercise from Jacques Lecoq, the French physical-theatre teacher (1921–1999), where instead of one person you have a chorus of three or four people and one main actor.

- Ask your group to split into groups of four or five.

- They are to create a scene in which one person is to act. They are given a basic theme and there is only a little discussion or preparation. The others act as chorus and provide the 'thoughts' and sound effects (doors opening/ phones ringing/ weather/environment, etc.) for one main actor. The chorus can speak individually or together.

- The chorus plays whatever the character might be thinking, which might be built from what the character is doing. For instance, if the actor walks around looking anxious, one of the chorus might say, 'You have nothing to worry about!' and a whole story might start from there. (See the example below.)

- The main actor should not speak too much. The text is mainly being supplied by the chorus.

- The chorus needs to be involved and focused on the main actor, perhaps being very close to them physically. It cannot be a free-for-all.

- After ten or fifteen minutes' work, each group shows to the others. These pieces are usually very amusing. Try and make sure the performers do not laugh.

Example scene:

ACTOR *walks around, agitated.* CHORUS *copy her mood, walking in all directions.*

1. Wait till she gets home.

2. Wait till they all get home!

ACTOR. Nooooo.

3. Will they ever forgive you?

   ACTOR *shakes her head furiously – looks at her phone, and out of the window.*

1. You want to call Jane.

2. Apologise.

3. Prepare them.

4. Forget it. It'll only make matters worse.

5. Much worse.

   ACTOR *puts the phone down.*

ACTOR. WHAT AM I GOING TO DO?

1. Everybody's going to hate you.

2. They ARE!

   ACTOR *looks at her hands. She goes to the sink.* 3 *makes running water sounds.*

1. You're a murderer!

2. The washing has all turned red.

3. You put it –

ALL. ON A BOIL!

3. Jane's dress is ruined.

ACTOR (*wailing*). It was an accident!

3. It's all your fault!

CHORUS *wail like distraught flatmates.*

1. And Siobhan's jeans...

2. You don't like Siobhan...

3. She never washes up!

ACTOR. I *do* like her.

(*Etc.*)

Clearly the group will not have their scene as tight as that, but do encourage them to be creative with sound. Let them all play with the scene and show it to the group. Suggest one improvement and then let them work for another five minutes. Do not allow the improvisation to go on too long. Let it have a beginning, a middle and an end. You might like to encourage them to write it down if you are going to spend a chunk of time on it.

This can be developed and written down, though when you do it is a challenge for everyone to maintain the sharpness and spontaneity. The chorus can develop a very distinct character, focusing not only on the lead actor but also speaking to the audience. There are many ways to develop this

Painting with Sound

I developed this idea when I was running some sessions with a youth theatre in an art gallery. Initially, don't give them too long with this creative exercise: about ten minutes so they do not have too long to think about it.

It can be useful to have some percussion instruments for this as well, though you do not want to overbalance the exercise and make it an excuse to bang a drum pointlessly. I find that, generally, if people are not used to working with instruments they can find them just another thing to worry about. If you have time, though, adding instruments might be a good move.

- Split the group into teams of about five.

- Hand out an A4 reproduction of a famous painting to each team. You might tell them what it is. Keep the picture a secret from the other groups.

- Tell them that what they have to do is create a soundscape with a beginning, a middle and an end, using the painting they have as an inspiration. In other words, they are going to be 'painting with sound'. It can have any kind of sound they want. They can use words and noises; for instance, if the painting is an impressionist painting they might want to make little pants to denote the dabbing of the brush. If the colour is green, they might want to intone 'green' on a low note. If there is a man fishing, someone might like to introduce the sound of the line swishing through the air and plopping into the water.

- Try and get them to have a shape to all of this as if it was a piece of music: this is quite important if they can manage it.

- Above all, it is important they try to get the *atmosphere* of the painting. Is it a scene of terror, of peace and serenity, of rich or poor – what? What movement might go with it?

- Ask them to present to the others. There is no right or wrong in this exercise, as long as it has some kind of shape, they use their voices, and what they show evokes something of the picture. Ask the rest of the group what kind of picture was suggested by the sound picture and then show the picture and see if it has any of those elements.

Animal

This is a wild game – loud, noisy and funny.

- Explain to the group you are going to pick two people, let's call them Cheryl and Patrick. They will each work alone to create an animal. It does not, and really should not, be a familiar animal. It is a fantasy creation of their own. The rest of the group stand on the periphery of the space.

- Stress it is important that no one gets the giggles (if possible).

- After the two people create their animals, tell them that they will then meet and respond to each other. They may like each other. They may not. Whatever happens they should just go with it. Tell the group that once the meeting of the animals gets going, you will come to someone watching and whisper 'Be a Cheryl', and the person goes and joins Cheryl as one of her species, and so on and so on until the whole group is working, some as Cheryls and some as Patricks.

- Ask Cheryl and Patrick to create their own animals and then meet.

- Usually their rhythms are quite dissimilar and they have certain attitudes about meeting. Let the others watch.

- Gradually add the rest of the group.

- Perhaps experiment with one group being much bigger than the other. Both groups instinctively find a character.

- Stop it once everyone has been added. If you do it again have the ones who entered last, enter first.

The Machines of Time and Place: A Use for Devising

When working on a Galway Youth Theatre production of *The Trial* by Steven Berkoff (after Kafka), we had many ensemble environments, rapid changes of scene and moods to create. We had to create the bank where Joseph K was working. We developed a complex set of movements, sounds and a rhythm circle, all emanating from the line, 'Good morning, can I help you?' to denote the mechanical and alienating life of the bank in which K works. By mixing those that spoke in rhythm and those that sang, and by altering the quality of sound, we made it sound appropriately discordant and nightmarish. This type of rhythm work is a brilliant way in which to create fantastic environments for the characters.

'Mary, Mary, Quite Contrary': Song as a Frame

The chances are, if you are devising, that you will need to create a framing device for a number of themed, related pieces of work that your young people have created. One of the best ways to do this is through a song, which is simple but can be altered in mood and atmosphere to end one scene and prepare the audience and performers for the next (one of the most important things a framing device has to do, in my opinion). As you have little time with your group, this framing device needs to be simple. If you look back at some of the movement work we did in conjunction with the simple song rounds, you might find some ideas there. A few years ago I worked with a mixed-ability group and we made a piece about growing older. We used the nursery rhyme 'Mary, Mary, Quite Contrary' as one of the main links, sung as a nursery rhyme, a rebellious teenage-punk version, a song of joy as someone gave birth, and a song of memory when someone was old. If you get your group vocally sensitive to atmospheres and qualities (the goal of so many of the basic exercises in this book), then you can use the same basic structure over and over and it will not get boring – because the quality or atmosphere will be completely different.

Ending the Session

A nice way to finish a more experimental session is with a lovely yoga exercise I learned when I was a young actor.

I cannot stress enough the importance of finishing a session well. It is comforting, uplifting and makes it part of a routine. It emphasises that we have all had an experience together.

So here is the exercise.

- Ask the whole group to kneel on the ground in a circle, with their buttocks on their heels if they can.

- You will need to show them the next part. Lean forward from the hips so that your face is near the floor, and your tummy is on your knees. Your hands should be relaxed and by your sides.

- Breathe in from the floor almost like you are an animal at a watering hole, sipping in some life-giving water.

- As you do this, start to come up from the hips, keeping your back straight, head tilted slightly upwards. Let your mouth be open and the jaw relaxed.

- Push the breath gently from your tummy and sing/intone an 'AHHHH' sound.

- As you make the sound, start to slowly come back down to the original position, so it is time to breathe in again just as you reach it. You then breathe in and repeat the breath out and the movement.

- Explain that everyone has different breath capacity so people will start and end at different times.

- If you are physically able to do this exercise, then do it with the group. When you think it appropriate, try to bring the group to a harmonious stop by saying 'One last round' – so that everybody waits in the down position, tummy on knees, until all have finished. If necessary, they can use one or two clenched fists to form a prop for their heads in the resting-down position.

Part 3

The Micro Sessions

Part 3
The Micro Sessions

'Had we but World enough, and Time…'

Andrew Marvell

In case you cannot do long sessions for whatever reason, Part 3 provides you with some short, thematic, fifteen-minute sessions that have a sense of wholeness about them; they are more to do with ritual and practice than working imaginatively.

Let's imagine you have been able to do a few full sessions with your group and now you want to keep voice on the agenda so as to retain their interest and register its importance. This part of the book is for you.

Equally, if your group needs coaxing into some voice work, then these micro sessions might be a less-demanding and easier place to start.

Getting a real improvement in the voice does require *practice*, and yet in drama workshops you often hear people have done an exercise and get bored doing it again. A good way to convince them of the need for this practice is to ally it to what you might be doing if you were getting your body fit for a sport, or wanting to be proficient in playing a musical instrument. If humanly possible you have to make them love the repetition, through ritual, energy and a sense of humour – both theirs and yours.

If you are starting here, I would suggest you explain the importance of voice, and suggest that for the next few weeks you are going to spend fifteen minutes each week on it.

Some of the exercises that follow will be new and some have been covered in earlier sessions. However, all are given here in full since you may be using this section of the book as a starting point.

The first exercise is new, and I would advise you to start with this one each time.

Micro Session 1: A Bit of Everything

Mmmaaaah, Mmmeeeee, Mmmooooh

- Ask the group to stand in a circle, feet parallel, knees slightly bent, arms by their sides, looking ahead and being aware of themselves in their own body.

- Ask them to feel their feet and legs reaching into the ground.

- You will need to demonstrate what follows first yourself: keeping the shoulders relaxed, breathe down into the belly, then intone a long '*mmmaaaah*' as you slowly open the arms wide. Look out into the space and feel the sound filling the whole room.

- When you have finished '*mmmaaaah*', gradually bring the arms slowly back to the sides as you breathe in.

- When you breathe out, reach with the hands, keeping them shoulder-width apart, slowly to the ceiling and intone '*mmmeeeee*'. As you do this, take your gaze up beyond your hands to the sky. Make sure your shoulders are relaxed. When you have almost run out of breath, slowly bring your hands down by your sides, breathing in as you go.

- Now intone '*mmmooooh*' and slowly reach out in front of you. When you have almost run out of breath, bring the arms slowly back to your sides.

- Repeat the whole sequence twice more.

Tip: Don't go to the very end of the breath... Watch for shoulder and neck tension. You do not have to tense your body to send your energy out into the space. Keep it nice and easy.

Head Rolls

- Ask them to drop the head to the chest and then *very slowly* roll the head to the right, to the back, to the left and back to the front in a circle (x4 each way).

Tip: Tell them to check the jaw and shoulders especially as these are two of the main areas that harbour tension. Keep an eye out.

Shoulder Chugs and Rolls

These exercises are for relaxing the shoulders.

- To vary the tempo a bit, give the instruction, 'Shoulders *up*, shoulders *centre*, shoulders *down*' (x4) quite quickly, like a game.
- Then ask them to rotate the shoulders forward very slowly, and incorporate the whole body, almost like skiing in slow motion. Then ask them to take the shoulders back in a circle the other way. Fully engage the knees and lower body (x4 forward and back).

Hand Throwing

- Ask everyone to turn to the left and find someone to look at on the other side of the circle. Ask them to put their weight on the left foot and change their weight to the right foot, throwing their right hand as if they are throwing it to their partner.
- Ask them to count '1-2-3-4-5-6-7-8' aloud, sending the sound across to their partner. Do this vigorously. Then they must turn their bodies to the right and repeat. This is a good releasing exercise.

- Now ask them to do exactly the same, this time not as loudly – but still to feel their voices are going towards their partner.

T–L–D

- '*Tttt*' – '*llll*' – '*dddd*'. These are all tip of the tongue exercises.. Do each one three or four times, e.g. '*tttt tttt tttt tah*' (x4), Then '*llll llll llll lah*' (x4), etc.
- Then '*tttt llll dddd*' (x6).
- Then '*tttt llll dddd, llll dddd tttt, dddd tttt llll*' – imagine they're written in front of you, if that makes it easier (x4).
- Do '*bbbb kkkk*'. Notice how with '*buh*' the sound is focused at the front of the mouth. '*Kuh*' is at the back of the mouth. Try '*pppp*' and '*gggg*' similarly.
- Ask them to do '*buh duh guh*'/'*puh tuh kuh*', slowly at first to register the focus, and then speed up.

Tip: For these basic but crucial exercises, try and get them to express the sound with their bodies as much as they can. You need to lead. So, if you say '*tuh*' with a punch, it is different to how you will say it if you glide your hand slowly across your body. Keep it rhythmic and fun. Do the sounds with them, or with call and answer.

Hey Hey Hee Hee Hah Hah

- Get them to do some jumps to flex their feet. Then, to take a wide stance. Look across the circle. Have someone in their sights! Start *slowly*.
- All point with the right arm, and call across to someone '*HEY!*'
- Then take out the right arm and put in the left and call across '*HEY!*'
- Then reach to the right sideways with the right arm and say '*HEE!*'

- Then reach to the left sideways with the left arm and say '*HEE!*'

- Then with the right arm you reach to the ceiling and say '*HAH!*'

- Then with the left arm you reach to the ceiling and say '*HAH!*'

This is one round. Do eight to ten rounds so you have a chance to pick up speed! The exercise can be as fast or slow as you like. You can be as demanding as you feel appropriate – try and get people to bend their knees, stretch and focus beyond their hands, for instance.

Micro Session 2: Projection/Resonance

Mmmaaaah, Mmmeeeee, Mmmooooh

As in Micro Session 1 (page 190).

Resonance (1)

Before you start this series of exercises, you might explain that the more resonant the voice is, the less effort is needed for your voice to carry, the more interesting it sounds, the more powerful it will be, and the more you as a performer will be able to share your feelings and those of the character. Explain that the whole body is like an instrument to be played. Do these exercises with them.

- Move the hand to the top of the head. Breathe in. Focus on where the hand is and send the sound up there. Hum into the hand. Try and make the hand vibrate, with a '*MMMMMMMAAAAHHH*'. Direct the vibration there.

- Put the hand to the bridge of the nose. Breathe in. Hum into the hand. Try and make the hand vibrate, with a '*MMMMMMMAAAAHHH*'. Direct the vibration there.

- Put your fingers lightly to your lips. As you breathe out and start to hum, bring your hand from your lips to about a foot in front of you. Open the sound '*MMMMMMMAAAAHHH*'. Focus on the hand as if you were singing into a microphone.

- Now put the hand on the chest. Breathe in. Hum into the hand. Try and make the chest vibrate, with a '*MMMMMMMAAAAHHH*'. Direct the vibration there.

- Now ask them to see if they can direct the resonance into any of those four places, to move their hands and the sounds around; to play with '*MMMMMMMAAAAHHH*'. They breathe when they need to. Ask them what they notice. Where do *they* resonate best?

Resonance (2)

- Ask each person to put one hand to her lips and the other on her tummy. Ask them to take a breath and make a hum.

- Watching their fingers, invite them to move their hand away from their lips, stretching the arm, all the time imagining the breath is reaching their fingers. Ask them to imagine the air as a stream of gold or silver touching their fingers.

- When the hand is held out in front of them, ask them to take another breath and imagine the breath is going to the back of the room, like a golden stream from their mouths. They can slowly bring their arms down to their sides as they do this.

- Finally ask them to intone: 'If music be the food of love, play on', on one rich note.

- Ask them to repeat the line several times, taking breaths when they need to, gradually making the phrase more like real, impassioned speech, but still with sufficient resonance to fill the room. Be aware you might still have to say '1-2-3, Go!'

- Ask them what they found out.

Tip: This exercise really is helped by the power of their imaginations. Getting them to look at their fingers as they breathe out and move their hands really helps with this. Be aware of tension in the body. Make sure they understand they must breathe again before they speak the line or the line will peter out.

Hey Hey Hee Hee Hah Hah

As in Micro Session 1 (page 192).

Try and get them to sense a time to slow down the exercise and stop all together without you being involved. Allow them to stand there in silence for a few seconds.

Micro Session 3: Breathing/Floor Work

Mmmaaaah, Mmmeeeee, Mmmooooh

As in Micro Session 1 (page 190).

Easy Stretch

- Ask the group to knit their fingers together, and hold their hands in front of their chests; then, breathing in, ask them to turn their hands, and stretch up. As they breathe out, then need to bring the hands back to the starting position. Ask them to keep the stretches light (x4).

- Ask them to push their knitted hands out front and push the chest to the back. Try and get them to release tension, to let go (x4).

- Then ask them to reach down, hanging from the waist. Get them to breathe and let the weight of the body take the upper body further towards the floor. The legs should be straight and shoulder-width apart at least.

- All the time, ask them to *notice* their breath. Then, *very slowly*, ask them to bring themselves to standing, curling up the spine vertebra by vertebra. The head and neck should be the last to go into place.

Shake Out

- Shake out the body vigorously and let low sounds come from the body. Keep shaking the body vigorously for a good thirty seconds at least.

- Let everyone feel the tingling when they stop.

Floor Work

Floor work is tricky to do quickly, so I would suggest that you develop the practice within longer sessions if at all possible before you try and do this ten-minute abbreviated version. Please check out the long process in Core Session 1 (starting on page 40) and do that with them a few times before you speed up.

I am going to continue as if all are working from the lying position rather than standing or sitting. You might remind them that breath is the fuel for the body.

- Lying flat on the floor, ask them to feel their bodies on the floor, to be really *in* their bodies. Notice if they feel any tension there; if so, where is it? Direct their attention to it and ask them to say in their heads 'let go', and their tense tension will let go. Tell them that if there is any residue from the tension of the day left in their bodies they might like to think of it just seeping into the floor.

- Get them to lift their feet up gently, bring their knees up and put the soles of their feet flat on the floor so that their spines are almost fully on the floor. Tell them not to worry if their backs are *not* fully on the floor.

- Say you are going to ask them to 'breathe in for four, hold in for four, breathe out for four'. As they breathe in, they should curl their lower back upwards, bringing their hips off the floor. On *hold*, they stay there, and on the *out*-breath they bring the pelvis gently down. Do this three times, each time asking the student to curl more of the spine, and hence bring their hips further off the floor.

- Ask them to raise their shoulders from the floor, and when you click your fingers, they let them fall (x4).

- Then ask them to slightly raise their hands from the sides of their bodies, you click your fingers and they let them go (x4).

- Ask them to move their heads easily and gently from side to side. After a few seconds ask them to bring their heads back to centre.

- Ask them to place their hands on their tummies, remembering this is the belt line and *not* the ribs. Go round and check the position of their hands.

- Ask them to feel the breath streaming in through the nose, down into the lungs and as if it were going right into the belly. This will make the tummy fill up and the hands rise.

- Now ask the young person to very, very gently pull the stomach in and let the air out of the mouth. Allow just the sound of the air to come from the lips. Spend a few minutes with this, breathing in and out. Check out how people are doing.

- Ask them to imagine the rhythm of the ocean, emphasising slightly the out-breath as the 'tide' goes out.

- Now ask them to breathe into the belly for four (you count), hold for four, and then to let go, and this time to voice the sound quietly.

- Do this three more times, encouraging them to take more breath and push a little harder, making a little more noise. Do not allow them to shout though; they are making a vocal sigh.

- Ask them to breathe in for four, hold for four, out for four (x2).

- Then breathe in for six, hold for six, out for six (x2).

- Then breathe in for eight, hold for eight, out for eight (x2).

- Now ask them to fix on a spot on the ceiling and imagine the breath is going right down into the belly, the tummy muscles are pushing and the sound is coming from their mouths like a golden fountain of sound, out to the spot on the ceiling. This visualisation of a golden sound can work well. Tell them they are going to make the sound '*mmmmmmAAAAH*'. You need to assure them that this might take a bit of practice and not to be despondent or dismissive. You are trying to get them to explore the connection between the belly, breath and sound here. Make sure they do a substantial '*mmmmmm*' before they open out the sound (x4).

- If most of them seem to have it, then ask them to sing 'Helloooooooooooooooo' out to the same spot on the ceiling.

Tip: Notice if anyone changes their breathing when you ask them to speak a word. It is amazing how tension and shallow breathing kicks in, often instantly, as soon as speech is introduced. If you feel this is happening with a few in the group, then stay with sound only.

When they have completed these floor exercises, ask them to roll onto their side, stay in that position for a few seconds and then get up *slowly*.

Find the Sound

- Now ask the group to close their eyes. Try and keep the focused mood going if you can. Explain to them this is a game for listening.

- Explain that every person in the room is going to sing a '*mmmmmaaaaaahhhhhh*' sound. They can breathe whenever they like but they need to keep the sound going and keep their eyes closed.

- Make sure everyone has their eyes closed. This can be hard for some, so suggest they put a hand over their eyes if they have any trouble. While you are talking, you walk around the room. You explain that you are going to touch someone on the shoulder. When every person starts to make the '*mmmmmaaaaaahhhhhh*' sound, the person you have touched will instead sing a '*mmmmmeeeeeeeeee*' sound. So everyone but one person will be singing '*mmmmaaaaah*', and one person will be singing '*mmmmmeeeeeeeeee*'.

- The job of the '*maaaaahs*' is to find the '*meeeee*' with their eyes closed. Once the '*meeeee*' is found (the '*meeeee*' can also move around as well) anyone who finds her then needs to stay with her and change her own sound to '*mmmmmeeeeeeeeee*'. Eventually the whole room is full of people hanging on to each other singing '*mmmmmmmeeeeeeeeee*'.

- Once all are together, tell them you are going to clap your hands and everyone must open their eyes and keep the sound going. When they open their eyes, they will want to relax and giggle. Try and control that because it destroys the energy. If it happens, stop the exercise here.

- If it does work okay, call a name and they must, with eyes open, lead and change the sound and add a repetitive movement that goes with the sound; then all must follow; then call another who changes the sound and movement and all follow her; then another. Finally one more, and ask that person to bring the movement and sound to a close. All stop together.

You can experiment with *Find the Sound* (2), as described in Core Session 2 (page 67), if the group has succeeded at this basic one.

Micro Session 4: Radiating/Receiving/Projection

Mmmaaaah, Mmmeeeee, Mmmooooh

As in Micro Session 1 (page 190).

Head Rolls

As in Micro Session 1 (page 191).

Easy Stretch

As in Micro Session 3 (page 195).

Throwing the Ball

In a circle, the group is going to *mime* throwing and catching a ball to each other.

- The way we throw is important. You might need to refer here to the pictures on pages 52 and 53 in Core Session 1. The person must have one foot behind the other and be able to throw underarm with an easy swing.

- Start the throwing going by throwing the imaginary ball to a member of the group. When people throw, it is important they stay with their throwing arm extended, looking at the person they are throwing to and sending their energy towards them. This *extension* is important so the student can feel both that the movement is finished and that they have sent energy to the catcher.

- The person who catches must receive the ball whilst looking at the thrower so an exchange is made.

- Do not initially go too fast. Keep it smooth and steady. Practise and be precise with these movements. It might be easier, depending on the nature of the group, to work externally with the mechanics of the movement, rather than talking about sending your energy. People are often very reluctant to stay with their arm outstretched. They throw their energy out quickly and weakly. Point out how on stage it is terribly important to share and communicate with the other actors as well as the audience. This exercise helps us to do that.

- Ask them to add a sound when they throw. Let them use their own name. Get them to notice when they feel their voices do not reach their catcher. Explore for a second the *why* of that. Could it be they need more breath to project effectively?

Resonance (1) and (2)

As in Micro Session 2 (pages 193 and 194).

Micro Session 5: Diction

Mmmaaaah, Mmmeeeee, Mmmooooh

As in Micro Session 1 (page 190).

Leg Throw

Get them to kick out with '*HAH!*' then a '*HEE!*' then a '*HO!*' Do it four times, kicking out faster each time.

Balancing Act

Balance has an extremely important effect on our confidence, our contact with the earth and our ability to speak clearly. Just ask them to stand on one leg and try balancing. Get them to move their bodies around. Suggest they try to change the tempo of the movement as they move, still trying to balance on one leg. Then ask them to change legs and repeat.

Diction Warm-Up

- *Shampoo.* Ask them to massage their scalps vigorously as if they are washing their hair (for young people who just did their hair this can be challenging!). Get them to massage into their necks too and even the shoulders a little.

- *Massage the jaw.* It might help for them to re-imagine the melting of the hinge of the jaw we did earlier.

- *Rinsing.* With hands on the face, get them to draw down their hands vigorously as if they were getting water off it Get them to make a '*fuh*' sound as they do it (x4).

- *Blow through the lips* (twenty seconds). Really loosen the lips.

- *Tongue flicking.* Flick out your tongue like a lizard (x4).

- *Chew fast/chew slow.* The change of tempo is good. Again, it reminds the whole being how different a feeling a new pace can give you.

- *Tongue circles.* Circle the tongue each way with the tongue on the outside of the teeth (x4). Then repeat, but this time on the *inside* of the teeth (x4).

- *Tongue directions.* Tongue to your nose/to your chin (x4).

- Tongue across side to side (x4).

- *Rubber face.* Put your fists in front of your face, then, as if you are stretching the face, pull the fists apart and stretch the face horizontally like a rubber mask. Bring your hands together, then pull them vertically and stretch the face vertically. Now try on the diagonal, both ways.

- Rinse the face again to finish.

T–L–D

As in Micro Session 1 (page 192).

A Fun Tongue-Twister

Do it line by line:

> 'Mr Chop the Butcher shuts his shop shutter
> Or perhaps his assistant shuts his shop shutter.
> The butcher's shop shutter
> Is a short sharp shutter
> And the butcher's short sharp shutter
> Should shut sharply.'

Hey Hey Hee Hee Hah Hah

As in Micro Session 1 (page 192).

Micro Session 6: Imagination and Voice

Mmmaaaah, Mmmeeeee, Mmmooooh

As in Micro Session 1 (page 190).

Consonant Characters

- Ask the group to find their own space and tell them you are going to say a consonant, let's start with 'puh'. Everyone is going to say 'puh' and keep saying it. Ask them how it makes them feel, and let the body go with the sound; in other words, they start to be the character of 'puh'. This is quite easy and nowhere near as 'out there' as it sounds. Get them to do this at the same time and work on their own or they might get giggly, and when they feel more comfortable, they can have a 'puh' party and relate to each other!

- Then change the sound to 'guh', 'vuh', 'buh', 'suh', 'ruh'.

Blue Voice, Green Voice

- Now ask them to imagine they have a centre in their belly which is *dark blue* and that their whole body is full of dark-blue energy. As they breathe out through their mouth, dark blue comes out. Ask them to really feel that: feel what it is like to have dark-blue breath and get them to make their breath audible.

- Then ask them to voice that blue sound. You might have to count down to a 'Go!' to set them off. Try and get them to simply say their name with that blue voice. If that goes well, try:

- 'It is spring, moonless night in the small town' (Dylan Thomas, *Under Milk Wood*). Have them repeat this line a few times.

- Then get them to take a breath in and shake out the whole body. This helps them to shed whatever the imagination brought up for them when they were working. It helps them to let it go.

- Try the same process with *orange*: hopefully the sound will be different. Don't forget to say '1-2-3, Go!'

- Breathe in/shake out.

- Now with *gold*.

- Breathe in/shake out.

Tip: I always check in with them after this kind of exercise to find out how they felt. I feel this is important because this ability to play with your voice is empowering and they need to articulate and 'name' it.

I hope these micro sessions will prove useful for you, especially with fledgling groups for whom a long session might be challenging. It is also good for those of you who want to provide a themed 'voice section' within a workshop to reinforce the idea that voice is something to be developed and valued. Micro sessions might even encourage practice!

Part 4

The Further Sessions

Voice in Productions

This short chapter explores some of the issues you might need to focus on when rehearsing a production with young people and incorporating voice into the work.

Whatever your circumstances, whether you are working in school, youth theatre, college or with a community group, many of the issues when you are directing a show will be the same. Whilst this chapter is primarily discussing how to integrate voice into the rehearsal process, some directing issues are going to come up as well, because it is almost impossible to separate acting from voice and other aspects of performance. They all influence each other.

Whatever piece you are doing you can never have enough time to rehearse. You may ask what possibility can there be for you to do some constructive voice work with the group? You are going to get this feeling even more strongly if you are new to directing, because directing is one of the most demanding managerial and creative roles any person can take on. On the other hand, paradoxically, you are going to have more contact time with your group when you do a show, so if you believe voice to be important, it is the ideal time to keep voice on the agenda. In some cases, connecting vocal practice to a show can be the key to really appreciating the value of the voice work done thus far.

There are a few other questions you might ask yourself when trying to accommodate voice work into a rehearsal schedule:

1. Why are you doing this play? What's the educational focus?

2. What kind of piece are you doing and what are the specific vocal demands this makes on the actors?

3. Where are you doing it and what are the issues with the venue, if any?

4. What type of group are you working with?

5. How long have you got to rehearse?

6. What skills do you need to give them? Does voice need to be high on the agenda?

Let's go through these one by one:

1. Why are you doing this play?

What is the focus? Is it *primarily* for them to have an experience, or to make work as good as they can produce? I would argue that, whether it is an end-of-term musical or a devised youth theatre project, there is no point throwing a young person onto the stage just for an experience with few skills to support them, whatever the aims are. It could be excruciatingly embarrassing for them. Therefore, for me, I think it is essential at least that every single person can be heard, and the more voice work you can fit in, the more chance you have of helping the young performer to be as expressive as they can, at whatever stage they are. We owe it to our groups to help them to be as good as they can be.

2. What are the vocal demands?

The demands on the voice are going to vary immensely depending on the type of play you choose. When doing Shakespeare with young people I invariably try to incorporate a number of voice workshops before rehearsals begin, not only on technique but also on the imaginative demands the language makes. Some of the basic work is in this book (particularly in the core sessions). If you were doing a naturalistic play you might be advised to do a lot of the work in Themed Session 5: Getting Real, in addition to the basic breathing and diction work.

3. Where are you doing it and what are the issues with the venue?

How big is the venue? What are the acoustics like? Is the hall/theatre prone to echo? If it is, then it is useful for the actors to use slightly less breath but enunciate very clearly. If you work in an echoey space, they need to do a *lot* of diction work. If the space is like speaking into a duvet, by which I mean very dry and flattening to the voice, they are going to have to project more and be more creative with pitch, which means using more breath. That kind of venue can really drain the voice of feeling and power, challenging even the most proficient speaker.

This is hard to gauge by just looking, and you and a colleague need to work this out by experiment.

Ask your colleague to move around the auditorium to different spots whilst you stay on the stage and try and speak to her. Try different sound levels and ask the colleague how much she can hear, so you get a sense yourself of what the challenges are. Remember, of course, that once the auditorium is full the acoustic is somewhat different. Echoes will be muted, but a challenging 'duvet' space will be even more challenging with an audience in it. Watch out for spaces with a wide playing area and a shallow auditorium too, as actors on one side or the other of the acting space need to project a lot further than they think. Remember that projection is not just about breath and clarity but also radiating your energy. (This issue of radiating is discussed many times in this book, but especially in Themed Session 2: Can You Hear What I'm Saying?)

This all presumes you are working in a theatre at all. Many youth groups produce amazing work in *site-specific* spaces, which are often quite small, and lessen the need to prioritise serious voice work. It is an attractive way to move towards the group's natural strengths. One of the most impressive proponents of this work is the acclaimed Irish director Louise Lowe, whose early work with the Ballymun Youth Theatre in Dublin led on to a whole range of exciting site-specific work, where small audiences were led into rooms to watch a young actor performing a short dramatic scene. However, this approach does not mean a group that creates work in this way should ignore voice altogether, because it is such an important and nuanced tool for communication. It just makes it less of a focus for the project in hand.

4. What type of group are you working with?

Who are your group? How much voice work have they done and what might be their attitude towards it? I would suggest that, whatever their level, some voice work is good or they will not be heard, and that, above all, is crucial. Light and regular warm-ups are good to get the breathing going and give them a sense of teamwork. You can make the work as light as you wish as long as you do *something*.

5. How long have you got to rehearse?

If, as I suggest, you incorporate a short warm-up at *all* group rehearsals, you are going to encourage the idea that voice is important for the group. Do not feel you are wasting your time; you are giving them the skills they need to make a good performance. This might be harder to justify for rehearsal calls of scenes with only two or three performers, but with these smaller scenes I try and get young actors to come early and warm up individually before the rehearsal begins.

The truth is that you are more than likely to feel squeezed as time goes on and eventually your warm-ups, both physical and vocal, might get diluted. Keep them going as frequently as you can and use anything such as a group song or chant in the show/piece as a warm-up opportunity.

6. What skills do you need to give them?

If we have addressed the above questions, then the answer to this one should be fairly easy to answer. Do not be overly ambitious. Obviously the audience needs to be able to hear them, but whether you focus in addition on feeling and diction or pitch or a sense of realism, don't overstretch yourself or your young actors. They will only be able to take in so much and you need to gauge it.

Tips

- You need to try and get ahead of the project before rehearsals start, and start teaching some of these skills before you start rehearsals. This is especially true of anything vocally demanding.

- Be selective with what you are trying to achieve. For instance, once when directing a youth theatre production of *A Midsummer Night's Dream*, I decided that a full expression of the language was the most important exploration we could do – not so much an *academic* one but an *emotional* one. This sometimes meant that the group over-projected slightly, but this was a very conscious trade-off in terms of the learning goals of the production. The confidence with the language affected their performances strongly and this in turn developed their physicality and released their general energy.

- This is really something that follows on from the last point: voice is less important in some types of production. When working on a youth theatre production of *The Trial* by Steven Berkoff after Kafka, the group had to focus most strongly on physical characterisation, atmosphere, ensemble work and movement. This did not mean we did not approach voice work but it was not as high a priority.

- You might consider working in chorus, which makes a lot of voice work easier because the young actors really feed off each other, and tend to become braver and more open. One of the great bonuses of directing a youth group is that you usually have a lot of people, and the buzz of speaking in a group can be very powerful. Perhaps explore adapting the script you are working with to accommodate this possibility. A good example of a recent youth theatre play actually written with a strong chorus is *Girls Like That* by Evan Placey, or my own play *Alien Nation* (see Bibliography).

- If the role is vocally demanding, you need to make sure you have someone who is up to that challenge, no matter how much they may suit the role emotionally or physically. If you cannot hear an actor you have a problem. As a general tip, you need to cast people, especially in main roles, who are going to show up at rehearsals and who are going to work. Unreliable people, however good they are, are a serious liability.

- Get as many rehearsals in the venue in which you are going to perform as you possibly can, to get the cast used to it and for you to assess the vocal challenges within the space.

- When working on a musical, make sure that the actors do not lose energy and breath when a song is finished and they go back to the dialogue. This is often a big problem in professional musicals too. This change of gear always feels to me like a messy landing in a plane. Remember the dialogue is as important as the song and there needs to be a smooth transition if the actors are to serve the story.

- If I feel some young actor has a particular vocal issue that is stopping them from performing well, I will take rehearsal time to work on it, and give the person an individual call. I find this is always appreciated, can be of assistance and makes them work harder on the issue.

- Always instill in the group that it is vital to do a warm-up before a performance, just as if they were going on to play a sport. Make sure it happens, if only for ten minutes.

Developing the Work

This final chapter explores and makes suggestions for further developments of the work, both for your group and yourself.

So far in this book I have only taken aspects of the voice work to an introductory level. This is because I know your time may be very limited with your group and your own expertise may need to develop gradually.

Structurally, only the core sessions have a strong, particular progression from one session to the next. The themed sessions could be done in any order you like. You might feel that some of what I have already suggested is overambitious for your group or your time frame – and that's fine. Use what you can. There is plenty in here for all types of groups.

So let's suppose that you teach the same group for some considerable time and you would like to develop the breathing and other voice work a little further. This is the scope of this chapter.

Before we start, I cannot stress how important it is to do some of your own personal work (a helpful starting point is described in the Introduction) and participate in sessions, even if you can only manage short ones, to augment your own experiential learning. At the end of the book there are contact emails for international teachers who work with voice and Chekhov Technique in particular, and your own national youth theatre organisations to suggest courses for facilitators.

Areas for Development

Development of Breathing

I have been very basic with the breath work for you and the group up to now, because it depends both on your own level and on the amount of time you have to focus on the work. The basic practice delivers confidence, relaxation and a clearer voice. That is a big reward in itself.

I have not, up to this point, focused on any rib breathing because, as I explained in the early sessions, it can create tension in young people of limited experience. There are some introductory exercises for rib breathing in this section you might like to try.

You might like to add the following exercises *after* the basic breathing work, but I would not advise proceeding with this more advanced work until they have practised the earlier core breathing for a few weeks. Make sure they know that if they get tired or dizzy, they must stop and rest.

Calling from the Belly

This exercise is especially useful when working on a piece to be performed in the open air or if they have to shout a lot in a play.

- With the young people in the lying position – knees up, feet flat on the floor – ask them to lift their heads a little from the floor, as if they were doing a crunch in the gym. Ask them to feel their tummy muscles, which will be tense. Ask them to lie down again and let the tummy muscles relax. Remind them that these muscles are the source of the voice power.

- In the lying position, ask them to put their hands on their tummies again and then to breathe into the belly as before.

- Start them off pulling the tummy in gently and then ask them to pull a little more firmly. The aim is to try and get them to pull the tummy in strongly so a loud sound comes from their mouths, rather akin to a shout. Use '*hah*'. At the start, though, it is just a pant. As they pull the tummy in more strongly the '*hah*' sound gets louder. This is a loud noise ideally made with the rest of the body completely relaxed, which enables the actor to shout without hurting her voice or tensing her shoulders.

- What you will notice is that they may start to use the ribs more or tense up. If that happens, ask them to 'let go', breathe and start again quietly.

- Once they get the hang of this (it may take several sessions) they can then explore sounds, pitches and tones whilst still keeping the power coming from the belly. This is most exciting when people realise they can make loud varied sounds in a relaxed way and they often get the giggles.

- You can then add words or short phrases.

- Progressing further, you can try and explore this exercise standing up.

More Fuel for the Body: Increasing the Breath to 10

Refer back to this exercise in Core Session 1 (page 44). Remember, though, that even when taking bigger breaths, they need to keep their body easy, so it is not sensible to progress to a ten count unless you have prepared the way with earlier exercises.

- Ask them to breathe in for four, hold for four, out for four (x2).

- Then breathe in for six, hold for six, out for six (x2).

- Then breathe in for eight, hold for eight, out for eight (x2).

- Then breathe in for ten, hold for ten, out for ten (x2).

Advanced Breath to 2/4/4

You might tell them that, as few roles require you to deliver many lines from the floor, nor take so long with the breathing, you need to develop your technique further, keeping the same mechanism but breathing more quickly. This exercise quickens the *in*-breath to something more akin to everyday life.

Please note: Do not try this exercise unless you have spent a number of weeks with them doing the more basic work.

• Breathe in for two, hold for four, out for four (x4).

Ask them what they felt. They may tell you their ribs moved a lot and this, of course, is fine. When people start using diaphragmatic breath they sometimes tense their ribs to keep them still in order to concentrate more on the belly breath. Try and point this out if you see such tensing-up, because that is not what we want to happen. The ribs need to be relaxed and will move, but they must not be the focus of the breath. If at this stage you want to explore rib breathing, here are a few old faithful exercises:

Gasp!

• Ask the group to each take in a big breath and slowly breathe out until there is no more breath left.

• As they get to the end of the breath, the reflex of gasping then kicks in and the floating lower ribs open widely. (It is astonishing how many people will tense up before the reflex but most people will feel the ribs move.)

• Ask them if they felt the ribs moving.

Basic Rib Breathing

• In the lying position with knees up, feet flat on the floor, ask the group to put their hands against the lower (or floating) ribs and to focus the breath there. Ask them if they feel the ribs moving. They will. Many people breathe here all the time.

• The problem with focusing on the ribs, from an acting point of view, is that the ribs alone do not give you much capacity, which means you have to take a lot of breaths and are in more danger of shallow breathing, thereby pushing and hurting your voice. You may or may not feel it appropriate to explain this.

• Try an 'in for four, hold for four, out for four' into the ribs with the hands on the lower ribcage at the front of the body (x4).

- Ask them to stand and work in pairs with someone they feel comfortable with. One stands behind the other and puts their hands on the lower ribs of the person in front. To be clear: this is about two inches above the waist. Have the front person breathe into their ribs and the other person feel it. Swap over. So much of this work is about getting to know your body and how it works.

Rib Breathing: How Rib and Belly Combine

Having come this far, it might be worth showing them how the rib and belly techniques combine. But I want to stress that as you are not training them to be actors you are only doing this to *explore*. If you can get your group to breathe from the belly for some parts of performances and practise it for relaxation, you will have triumphed. Exploring rib work is the icing on the cake!

- In the lying position with knees up, feet flat on the floor, ask each person to put one hand against the lower (or floating) ribs on one side and the other on the tummy.

- Ask them to breathe into the tummy but let the ribs expand as well.

- Breathe out. Do this a few times.

- Now ask them to breathe into the tummy for four, into the ribs for four then pull the tummy in for four, then let the ribs go down for four (x4).

- The good thing about exploring this is it reassures them that the ribs have a *function* in breathing.

Development of Resonance

You might like to remind your group that they are playing their body and the whole being like a musical instrument. In addition to working on the resonators at the top of the head, the nasal passages, the lips and the chest, described in Core Session 1, here we are going to explore resonators in other parts of the body.

- Ask each person to put a hand at the back of the head, breathe in and hum, bringing the sound gradually to an '*ahhh*'. At the same time ask them to direct the sound to the hand; to feel the vibration on the hand. A good tip is to relax the jaw.

- Then move the hand to the top of the head, breathe in, and hum again. Ask them to note how the texture and tone of the voice changes.

- Now put the fingers of each hand to the cheeks, open the mouth and smile. Breathe in. Try and make the fingers vibrate.

- Swallowing first, put the hand gently against the throat, breathe in, and *very gently*, ask them to direct the sound there, again with a '*mmaaaahh*'.

Development of Exercises from Themed Sessions

The following exercises/games are linked to related exercises in particular sessions, so if you are working specifically with rhythm, say, and you need a more demanding exercise for your group, you might find it here.

Opera! (leading on from Themed Session 1: Wake the Word)

This exercise is fun, but you need a brave group to do it, otherwise it just dissolves in hysterical giggles. It's noisy too. It is kind of a lead-on from the early session where you sing 'Happy Birthday' in different styles. When it works well it explores mood, rhythm and sound.

- Split them into groups of three to five people. Ask them to create a short scene which can be about anything they like, but they have to sing it. The style of singing needs to have something to do with the scene. For instance, if they are doing a scene about moving to the big city, they might try and sing as if they were in an American musical. If they were singing about the end of a love affair they might choose grand opera. If they chose a scene about someone finding someone else attractive they might try a pop-song style. The important thing is they do not have to be able to sing. They can play and send it up as much as they want, but they must try not to laugh.

- Give them ten minutes and then let them show their work to the rest of the group.

- Everyone more than likely will send it up. If you have a confident group you might ask one team to try and do something as an opera, but with a very serious story. Ask them to play it as seriously as they can. The impact of this can be quite amazing when it works, but there is no guarantee of success.

Polar Opposites (leading on from Themed Session 1: Wake the Word)

This exercise also requires a confident group and a reasonably sized space. The aim is to free people physically and get them responding and thinking about language. You can ask them to work in pairs, or have one pair work at a time and *side-coach* as they work (see note below). You might want to start off this way so you can show the whole group what they might aim for before you split them into pairs, it is up to you.

Please note: Side-coaching is when you give instructions whilst the exercise is going on. So as they work you might suggest an actor does something as they keep going. They take in what you say but they don't stop working and break the energy.

- Ask the pair to think about an opposite. Let's take 'hot' and 'cold'. You tell them one person is going to be hot and one is cold. Ask them to work on their own and really get those qualities into the body *physically*.

- Then tell them to start saying the word, influenced by the way they are moving, and start to relate and work with their opposite. They can only use the word they have been assigned.

- To begin with, each person tries to influence the other but sometimes the work develops more interestingly. Tell them that if they think of another meaning for the word, they can put that into their body and change the whole energy of the improvisation. For instance 'hot' can mean literally hot in temperature, hot property, the next big thing, physically attractive, and so on; 'cold' can mean distant, cold in temperature, superior, disappointed, etc.

- You can work with open/closed, in/out, up/down, full/empty, war/peace, big/small, and ask the group for suggestions.

I love this exercise because it unites body, voice and imagination in a very free and creative way. It shows us how words are multi-layered in meaning and we can explore that through voice and body.

It can be very useful to use this when exploring what the major polarities are in a play you might be working on. For instance, in *Girls Like That* by Evan Placey, an excellent youth theatre piece on cyber bullying, you could explore a whole series of polarities with this exercise: conforming/rebelling, freedom/imprisonment, teenager/adult, respect/contempt.

Tribals (1) (leading on from Themed Session 1: Wake the Word)

This is an exercise I learned from Bruce Myers, one of Peter Brook's actors. I later developed it as a more naturalistic chorus exercise but this is the exercise more or less as I first learned it. You need a lot of room for this. It helps to connect voice and body, requires discipline and yet is great fun. It also helps give less confident people a stronger sense that they can lead the group.

- Ask the group to make two teams and assign a leader to each. Choose confident leaders first. Let's call them A and B.

- Have the leaders stand facing each other a few feet apart. Tell them they are going to have a conversation in sound and movement.

- Ask the followers of each leader to make a straight line behind their leaders stretching across the space. They must be able to see someone in the other team directly opposite them. That is the person they are going to focus on, though they also need to see their own leader.

- Ask everyone to stand like their leader. Two tribes are now facing each other, each with someone in their sights.

- Leader A (looking at Leader B) makes a sound and a movement, maybe issuing a challenge. Leader A stays frozen when she is finished.

- Group A copies the movement and sound of their leader, focusing on the Group B member opposite them.

- Leader B (responding to Leader A) makes a gesture and a sound. It must be a *response* to what Leader A has done.

- Group B copies the movement and sound of their leader, focusing on the group A member opposite them.

- The cycle begins again. Allow about five exchanges, and then swap the leaders over. Give as many people the opportunity to be leader as you can.

Tips:

- Really try and promote the idea that the leaders respond to each other rather than just making aimless movement.

- Encourage brave, big moves and sounds.

- Make sure the movement isn't so physically ambitious that it involves too many fancy turns or the chorus will not be able to follow the leader.

Tribals (2) (leading on from Themed Session 5: Getting Real)

The exercise above has a very useful development where we use a real conversation between the leaders. It helps the participants really to *listen* to the tone and words without discussing it and enables them to get some more variety and tone into the voice. The rules stay the same: the two leaders are having a realistic conversation with a little movement, sitting/standing opposite each other, with their choruses behind them. Everyone has to sit/stand like their leader and move as they do.

Example scene:

LEADER A. Hi, Anna. (*Raising her hand.*)

GROUP A. Hi, Anna. (*Raising her hand.*)

LEADER B. I'm not talking to you. (*Turns away a little.*)

GROUP B. I'm not talking to you. (*Turn away.*)

LEADER A. Why not? (*Extends her hand.*)

GROUP A. Why not? (*Extend their hands.*)

LEADER B. YOU TOLD MY MOTHER! (*Throwing arms open.*)

GROUP B. YOU TOLD MY MOTHER! (*Throwing arms open.*)

And so on. You can change leaders and try different conversations.

Rhythm Development (leading on from Themed Session 3: I've Got Rhythm)

This exercise follows on from the rhythm work and was taught to me by Debra Salem, whom I mentioned earlier. It is rather hit and miss, but if you enter into it in a spirit of fun, having done the earlier workshop, it could be fabulous and go on for many minutes.

- Split the group into two lines against opposite walls.

- Each person devises their own sounds and tune to fit into a 4/4 beat (as in *Boom Chicka*, page 120). The tune can be as simple or as complicated as the participant wants. They sing their tune quietly to themselves until they have it solid. They walk into the centre and find another person, who is singing a tune/rhythm too. Each person listens carefully to the other as they continue to sing their own tune: as they progress they will start to compromise their rhythms with each other until they 'reach agreement' without discussion, singing their rhythms together. They will both need to adjust a little but with listening and faith it *will* happen! Tell them not to force the issue, just go with the flow.

- Then, with the pairs staying together with their newly adjusted tunes and rhythm, you start to guide them into groups of four. So each pair meets another pair and follows the same process, listening carefully to each other's tunes and rhythm and gradually folding their tunes and rhythms into each other. Tell them not to rush it.

- Once established, you bring a group of four to another four and they go through the same process. Finally, move the whole group together. This requires some serious listening. The whole room is all working in a complex way on a group piece.

- Build it up. Try conducting, bringing the volume up and down. Perhaps a tune will emerge. Conduct the whole group to quietness and silence.

- Bravo! When there is silence, try and hold it for a second.

Developing Working with Text

Change Thought, Change Direction

This is an extremely useful exercise should you have a group working on speeches of some length or when you are practising public speaking.

- Have each person facing in different directions; they are working 'alone, together'. Ask everyone to walk forward briskly as if they are really going somewhere. Now ask them to stop.

- Now ask everyone to fix on a spot ahead of them and get the feeling that they really want to walk towards it but they can't. Ask them to let that feeling grow and grow. You will find that they will start to sway a little if it is really working for them.

- Keeping that focus and intention, ask them to step forward. They might laugh. It feels strange. Ask them what they felt. If they felt nothing, the likelihood is they were simply engaging more with the head, asking themselves 'How do I do this?' 'What does the leader want me to do?' Maybe try it again and insist they consider nothing else but this impulse to walk forward. Explain to them that that is an *impulse*. They are going to explore that impulse through the text. Reassure them that there is nothing wrong with them if they do not feel an impulse. It just might take practice.

- Ask them to walk forward as they say their speech. Every time the character changes direction with the speech in *tone* or with a *new idea* they must literally do the same, change direction and walk.

- When they change direction, they might change the tone or speed of what they are saying and this is getting variety into the voice and body. Suddenly the speech will become enlivened.

- This is a great way to explore the thought processes and intentions of the character, which they can then commit to their playing of the text if it feels right.

Working with Text: Blood Wedding *by Federico García Lorca*

Lorca's classic (translated here by Jo Clifford) is a brilliant play to use for teaching because of its mixture of the poetic and the everyday, its extraordinary full-blooded passion, and its accessible characters, full of lust, frustration and rebellion.

Act One, Scene One

A room painted yellow.

BRIDEGROOM (*coming in*). Mother.

MOTHER. What?

BRIDEGROOM. I'm going.

MOTHER. Where?

BRIDEGROOM. To the vineyard. (*About to leave.*)

MOTHER. Wait.

BRIDEGROOM. What do you want?

MOTHER. I want to give you some food to take.

BRIDEGROOM. Don't bother. I'll eat grapes. Give me the knife.

MOTHER. Why?

BRIDEGROOM (*laughing*). To cut them off the vine.

MOTHER (*muttering as she looks for it*). Knives... knives... I curse them. Curse them all and the criminals who make them.

BRIDEGROOM. Let's talk of something else.

MOTHER. And machine guns and pistols and knives and sickles and scythes.

BRIDEGROOM. That's enough.

MOTHER. Everything with a blade that can cut open the body of a man. A beautiful man, with a mouth like a

226

flower. A man who goes out to his vines or his fields or his olive groves because they are his...

BRIDEGROOM (*lowering his head*). Be quiet. Please...

MOTHER....and then never returns. Or if he does, if he does come back it's only so we can cover his head with a shroud or cover him with salt to stop his corpse swelling. I don't know how you dare carry a knife in your belt or why I keep one in my house. It's like keeping a snake.

BRIDEGROOM. Haven't you said enough?

MOTHER. No. I'll never say enough. Not even if I lived to be a hundred. First they killed your father who smelt like a rose. I only enjoyed him three years. Then they killed your brother. And is it right and is it just that something as small as a pistol or a knife can finish off a man? A man is a bull, it should take more than such a tiny thing. So no. I'll never be silent. Months pass. Years pass, and despair bites into me. I can feel it gnawing. At the back of my eyes. At the roots of my hair.

BRIDEGROOM (*fiercely*). Will this never end?

MOTHER. No. No, this will never end. Can anyone bring your father back? Anyone bring back your brother? And people talk of jail. But what's that? They can eat there. The murderers. They can eat there, and smoke if they want, and play their guitars. And my two dead bodies turning into grass. Slowly turning into grass. With no voice in their heads. Only dust. Two men once fresh as flowers. While the murderers live in jail. Cool as cucumbers. With a view of the mountains...

BRIDEGROOM. So you want me to kill them?

MOTHER. No. No, I'm only talking because... They went out that door. How can I bear to see you go out of it too? And I don't like you carrying a knife. It's just... I hate you going out the house.

BRIDEGROOM. The nonsense you talk.

MOTHER. I wish you were a girl. Then you'd stay at home and we'd do the sewing together. We'd embroider tablecloths and knit woolly jumpers for the winter.

BRIDEGROOM (*taking the* MOTHER *by the arm, and laughing*). Mother, what if I took you with me to the vineyard?

MOTHER. And what would an old woman do in the vineyard? Would you lie with me under the grapes?

BRIDEGROOM (*picking her up in his arms*). You? You old old old old old woman, you.

MOTHER. Your father used to take me. Yes. There was a man for you. Good stock. Your grandfather left a child in every street corner. That's how it should be. Men being men. Grass being grass.

BRIDEGROOM. Mother. What about me?

MOTHER. What about you?

BRIDEGROOM. Have I got to explain it all over again?

MOTHER (*gravely*). That.

BRIDEGROOM. Do you think it's a bad idea?

MOTHER. No.

BRIDEGROOM. Well then?

MOTHER. I'm not sure I really know. You bring it up like that, all of a sudden, and it throws me. I know the girl is good. And that's right, isn't it? I know she's got good manners, and I know she's a good worker. She can bake her own bread and sew her own clothes and yet whenever I think of her name it's as if my head was being hit by a stone.

BRIDEGROOM. That's ridiculous.

228

MOTHER. No. It's not ridiculous. It's just I'll be left on my own. You're all that I've got left and I don't want you to go.

BRIDEGROOM. But you'll come with us.

MOTHER. No. I can't leave your father and your brother here on their own. I have to go and see them every morning. Because if I didn't, one of that family of murderers, one of the Felix, one of them could die and they might bury them beside my dead. And I couldn't bear that. Never. Never! Because I would have to dig them up with my fingernails and smash their bones against a wall.

BRIDEGROOM (*angrily*). And now you've started. Again.

MOTHER. I'm sorry. (*Pause.*) How long have you been seeing her?

BRIDEGROOM. Three years. Enough time to buy the vineyard.

MOTHER. Three years. Wasn't she once going to marry someone else?

BRIDEGROOM. I don't know. I don't think so. Girls have to think hard about who they're going to marry.

MOTHER. No. No, they don't. I never thought. I never looked at anyone. I looked at your father. And then when they killed him I looked at the neighbour's wall. A woman can have just the one man. And that's all.

BRIDEGROOM. You know that she's a good girl.

MOTHER. I'm sure she is. I just wish I knew who her mother was.

BRIDEGROOM. What difference does that make?

MOTHER (*looking at him*). My son.

BRIDEGROOM. Now what do you want?

MOTHER. To tell you you're right. That I believe you! When do you want me to call on them?

BRIDEGROOM (*happily*). What about Sunday?

MOTHER (*seriously*). I'll take her the brass earrings, because they're antiques, and you'll buy her...

BRIDEGROOM. You'll know what's best...

MOTHER. You buy her some fancy stockings, and two new suits for you... Not two. Three! You're all I have!

BRIDEGROOM. I'm off. I'll go see her tomorrow.

I devised this exercise to introduce young people to poetic text. It encompasses passion in the body and the voice, language, issues of story, putting scenes into broad sections, and identifying themes.

- First of all, read the scene all together sitting in a circle, each person reading a speech. Discuss the scene a little and introduce the world of the play to the group. What sort of feelings do they have about the world?

- Split the group into pairs and have them read the scene. This scene can easily be split in three sections:

  Section One: The initial altercation exposing the mother's grief and the son's desire to leave the house. It explores their mutual dependency and she tells us about the fact that her husband and other son were killed by a member of the Felix family, who is now in jail.

  Section Two: The son asks again his mother's feelings about him getting married, and virtually, her permission. She is reluctant to lose him and be alone, and suspicious of the prospective bride.

  Section Three: The mother agrees to go with him to discuss the wedding with the family and prepare for it.

- Once they have read the text tell them they have to act out the whole of this first scene using only four words, which they can repeat as many times as they like. This makes them question what is happening in the scene and what it is actually about. Four words that work well, though not the only four, are 'knife', 'marriage', 'family', 'alone'.

- They are then given ten minutes to work on this. Tell them they must not use the words like gibberish and that when they say them they must mean something. 'Family', for instance, refers not only to the mother but the son's desire for his own *family*.

- Show all the pieces and give feedback. Notice how using different words changes the interpretation and focus of the whole scene.

This can be extraordinarily intense and successful, partly because it encourages the actors to use pauses, as well as be very clear they are exploring the words for emotional and sense meaning.

Working with Text: One to One

Finally, I want to explore how you might help an individual member of your group with a speech or scene. The good thing about this is you can focus on their own particular issues rather than worry about the other actors in the scene. They feel less embarrassed if they are floundering and you can really give them space to work. It makes them feel they are not alone and if they are aware they are having a problem they feel supported.

The first thing you need to consider is the *type* of young actor you are dealing with, their experience, and what the best approach needs to be in order to be the most helpful. Are you going to approach the poem/speech from the imaginative or the technical route to begin with? Where might the performer be most comfortable to start? Let's imagine you start with the technical work first, though it is not always the best way round.

Stage 1: Technical Work

Let's say you are working with The Singer's Speech at the end of Part Two of *The Caucasian Chalk Circle* by Bertolt Brecht (a wonderful play to do with young people). In the speech, The Singer tells us of the servant girl, Grusha, who decides to save a baby, which will undoubtedly be killed if it is found. Grusha acts out much of what is described as the Singer speaks. Here it is:

THE SINGER.
As she was standing between courtyard and gate, she heard
Or thought she heard, a low voice. The child
Called to her, not whining but calling quite sensibly
At least so it seemed to her: 'Woman', it said, 'Help me'.
Went on calling not whining but calling quite sensibly:
'Don't you know, woman, that she who does not listen to a cry for help
But passes by shutting her ears, will never hear
The gentle call of a lover
Nor the blackbird at dawn, nor the happy
Sigh of the exhausted grape-picker at the sound of the Angelus.'
Hearing this

(GRUSHA *walks a few steps towards the* CHILD *and bends over it.*)

she went back to the child
Just for one more look, just to sit with it
For a moment or two till someone should come
Its mother, perhaps, or someone else –

(*She sits down opposite the* CHILD, *and leans against a trunk.*)

Just for a moment before she left, for now the danger was too great
The city full of flame and grief.

(*The light grows dimmer as though evening and night were falling,* GRUSHA *has gone into the palace and fetched a lamp and some milk, which she gives the* CHILD *to drink.*)

Terrible is the temptation to do good!

(GRUSHA *now settles down to keep watch over the child through the night. Once, she lights a small lamp to look at it. Once, she tucks it in with a brocade coat. Now and again she listens and looks up to see if someone is coming.*)

For a long time she sat with the child.
Evening came, night came, dawn came.
Too long she sat, too long she watched
The soft breathing, the little fists
Till towards morning the temptation grew too strong.
She rose, she leaned over, she sighed, she lifted the
    child
She carried it off.

(*She does what the* SINGER *says as he describes it.*)

Like booty she took it for herself
Like a thief she sneaked away.

Let's imagine you choose to approach the piece in a technical manner first, looking at where she might breathe and what words are important to emphasise in order to better be able to communicate the sense. This is more in the area of speech and drama, and whilst not valueless, it is far from everything.

However, let's say you have started there and you have a young actor who is now reading intelligently but with little or no feeling or intention.

Stage 2: Atmospheres and Qualities

Let's now do a little work using Chekhov's concept of Atmospheres and Qualities, which we have touched on elsewhere in Core Session 2.

• Ask the actor to try to define what is the main atmosphere of the piece, in other words what feeling surrounds the piece of text. She might say: 'danger', 'fear', 'worry', to name but a few.

- Pick one of these words to work with; let's say 'danger'. Ask the actor to imagine that the atmosphere of the piece is *danger*, to close her eyes, and imagine the whole room is filled with an atmosphere *of danger*. Ask her to breathe it in and 'turn it up' quite strongly. Ask for details like: 'What does it smell like?' 'Does it have a colour?' 'Does the feeling in the atmosphere push you forward or back?' 'Does it press you down or pull you up?' Then ask her to speak the lines. If she does not know them, just feed her a couple quite flatly and ask her to repeat them. This can produce some powerful results, with the text and voice infused with a palpable sense of danger; the breathing changes. Of course, it is more useful if the actor knows a few of the lines.

- Do not be concerned that the young actor is going to be stereotypically afraid. First of all, when you say 'danger', every single person's response to what this atmosphere of danger might be like is quite nuanced. However, provided she is responding to this atmosphere and not letting her intellect get in the way, then this sense of danger will be truly felt and expressed.

- When you have explored this a little, get the actor to open her eyes and *shake out thoroughly.* It is very important to do this. Remind the actor they are getting rid of the feeling!

- However, danger may not really be the word I would be looking for here, though it's a strong one and easy to produce. I might suggest an atmosphere of 'compassion' that is all around her and filling the whole room. Again ask, 'What does that feel like?' 'Is it warm or cold?' 'What does it feel like on your skin?' Ask her to breathe it in. Get her to try a few lines. After she has done this, ask her to see if she can also speak with the emphasis and breathing which she has done on the piece earlier, whilst maintaining the compassionate atmosphere. Some people find this hard, others easy.

Interestingly, you might find that the emphasis and breathing will change with the created atmosphere, and that is fine too, if it works for actor and director. Importantly, whether either of these atmospheres is 'right' is not the point. You will find the right one through experimenting.

What we are getting at here is something far, far deeper, than intellectual sense. If the young actor is connected to their body this work can be intense, so you need to be a little cautious. That's why shaking it out thoroughly is important.

Stage 3: Working with Gesture

Working with gesture might be a more effective way for some people to achieve a similar result. Again, this is work we have touched on in other sessions (*Verbing the Body* in Themed Session 1, page 93). It is, fundamentally, Chekhov's Psychological Gesture.

- Tell the young actor that we are looking for the *intention* of the speech and we are going to find this in the body through gesture. Ask her to keep both feet on the ground, one foot behind the other, and imagine she is pulling something with both hands towards her. It works much better if you commit the whole body to the action. Ask her to keep repeating this gesture and she will start to get a sensation, which will give her a feeling. You don't need to explain this.

- Ask her to make a sound as she is pulling, and on the bedrock of that sound to introduce the text. The text is not a strong pull but could be a soft, gentle one, almost an enticement to the audience to listen to what is coming next.

Physicalising intention gives a strong focus to the quality of the language and is far more nuanced than a primarily intellectual approach.

The next stage is to use the gesture *and* the atmosphere together for a truly nuanced mix, but adding both might be too difficult. Try only as much as they can manage. The unconscious aim of so much artistic work is complexity. My feeling is that with simplicity, the complexity will come.

In Conclusion

I hope you find this book useful, that it has opened up your own ability to explore your own voice, and that it has given you more strategies and confidence in working with voice with your own groups of young people.

I hope it has transmitted some of my love of working with the voice, its value, and that it has given you a number of tools with which to work.

Here are a few key things I would like you to remember now you have finished this book and hopefully tried out the exercises:

- It is more productive and more fun to free the body, imagination and voice *together*, as this can free the whole person.

- Try to remember your goals as teacher/facilitator. Are you *introducing* your group to voice fundamentals or are you trying to give them serious *proficiency* as well?

- Remember that this work should be joyous and liberating, and that repetition, which helps promote a sense of group identity, can be fun.

- Remember to instil in the group that this great instrument of voice helps them not only to be better actors but more rounded and relaxed human beings. Remind them that voice is useful for many professions, as well as in college and at school.

- Remember that good acting is not just about speaking but listening, receiving and responding.

- Remember to *breathe*.

I would like to conclude by reminding you of the quote from Michael Chekhov's *Lessons for Teachers* that appears as the epigraph for this whole book:

> 'If you are teaching, you must be active.
> You must not give the impression of activity.
> You must be active...
> Try to speak as if from your whole being.'

Appendices

Bibliography

Books

Belloc, Hilaire (1991) 'Tarantella' in *Complete Verse*, London: Pimlico.

Brecht, Berthold (1963) *The Caucasian Chalk Circle*, trans. Auden, Stern and Stern, London: Methuen Drama.

de la Mare, Walter (1954) 'The Listeners' in *The Golden Treasury*, selected by F.T. Palgrave, London: Collins.

Eliot, T.S. (1935) *Murder in the Cathedral*, London: Faber and Faber.

Hafler, Max (2002) *Alien Nation* in *Playshare Volume One: A Collection of Plays for Young People* (2005), Dublin: National Association for Youth Drama.

Hafler, Max (2009) *This Means War!*, unpublished play for Galway Youth Theatre, Cúirt Festival, Galway.

Lorca, Federico García (2008) *Blood Wedding*, trans. Clifford, Jo, London: Nick Hern Books.

O'Rowe, Mark (1997) *Buzzing to Bits* in *Playshare Volume One: A Collection of Plays for Young People* (2005), Dublin: National Association for Youth Drama.

Placey, Evan (2014) *Pronoun*, London; Nick Hern Books.

Placey, Evan (2013) *Girls Like That*, London: Nick Hern Books.

Poliakoff, Stephen (1976) *Hitting Town and City Sugar*, London: Eyre Methuen.

Quercus (2005) *Speeches that Changed the World*, London: Quercus Publishing.

Shakespeare, William, *Macbeth* (*The Arden Shakespeare*), ed. Kenneth Muir, Walton-on-Thames: Thomas Nelson.

Thomas, Dylan (1954) *Under Milk Wood*, London: J.M. Dent.

Yousafzai, Malala: Speech to the United Nations, July 14th 2013.

Films

Shakespeare in Love (1998), directed by John Madden, Universal Films.

Books to Expand Your Teaching

Berry, Cicely (1973) *Voice and The Actor*, London: Virgin Publishing.

Brook, Peter (1998) *Evoking (and Forgetting) Shakespeare*, London: Nick Hern Books.

Callery, Dymphna (2001) *Through the Body: A Practical Guide to Physical Theatre*, London: Nick Hern Books.

Case, Sarah (2013) *The Integrated Voice: A Complete Voice Course for Actors*, London: Nick Hern Books.

Chekhov, Michael (1991) *On the Technique of Acting*, New York: HarperCollins.

Chekhov, Michael (2000) *Lessons for Teachers of His Acting Technique*, Ottawa: Dovehouse Editions Inc.

Chuen, Master Lam Kam (1991) *The Way of Energy*, London and Stroud: Gaia Books.

Hughes, Langston (1954) *The Book of Rhythms*, New York: Oxford University Press.

Linklater, Kristin (2009) *Freeing Shakespeare's Voice: The Actor's Guide to Talking the Text*, London: Nick Hern Books.

Contacts

Further Learning and Organisational Support

National Association of Youth Drama Ireland **www.nayd.ie**

National Youth Council of Ireland **www.youth.ie**

Youth Theatre Arts Scotland (development organisation for youth theatre in Scotland) **www.ytas.org.uk**

National Association of Youth Theatres (development organisation for youth theatre in England) **www.nayt.org.uk**

Ulster Association for Youth Drama (development organisation for youth theatre in Northern Ireland) **www.uayd.co.uk**

A few other ones for you to look at...

Scottish Youth Theatre **www.scottishyouththeatre.org**

National Youth Theatre **www.nyt.org.uk**

Artswork **www.artswork.org.uk**

Teachers of Chekhov and Voice

If you are interested in developing your voice work in the way described in this book, here are the contact emails some teachers (including myself) who teach both Voice and Chekhov Technique.

Max Hafler, Galway, Ireland **maxhafler@icloud.com**
www.maxhafler.wordpress.com

Sarah Kane, London, UK **sar.kan@hotmail.com**

Craig Mathers, Boston, USA **craig_mathers@emerson.edu**

John McManus, New York, USA
shakespearealive@gmail.com

Suzana Nikolic, Zagreb, Croatia **suzana@adu.hr**

Chekhov Training Organisations

These are the organisations of which I have the most experience who run courses, one based in Europe, the other in the United States.

The Michael Chekhov Association **www.michaelchekhov.org**

Michael Chekhov Europe **www.michaelchekhoveurope.eu**

Sample Voice Sheet for Young People

Here are some basic exercises which might run into a ten-minute programme. Try and do it every day. Also available as a free download at www.nickhernbooks.co.uk/teachingvoice

Breath

BREATH IS THE FUEL FOR EVERYTHING YOU DO.

It carries everything; our actions, our *feelings*, our words.

You need to be able to control your breathing so that the way you phrase speeches will be under your control.

- Lie on the ground, knees up, feet flat on the floor. Relax. Breathe into your whole body and sigh out. When you breathe in, imagine your whole being is softening and lightening. Ask yourself, 'Where does the tension sit in my body? Is it the shoulders?' If so, move them slightly. Feel all the tension falling into the floor.

- Now put your hands lightly on your tummy. Breathe in. Feel the breath going through the nose and right down under your hands. That is not what is really happening but it helps to imagine it like that. (It's the large diaphragm muscle moving down which makes the tummy expand.) Now breathe out through the mouth, pulling the tummy in gently as you do.

- Take a number of breaths in this way and, as you breathe out, voice them softly with a soft 'ahh' sound.

- Whilst the ribs are important, try and focus more on the tummy and breathe 'into' it. The tummy expands when you breathe in.

- Ask them to breathe in for four, hold in for four, out for four (x2).

- Then breathe in for six, hold in for six, out for six (x2).

- Then breathe in for eight, hold in for eight, out for eight (x2).

- Still on the floor, exercise the diaphragm. Pant lightly by pulling in the stomach, then relax. Breathe in and repeat the process. Don't worry necessarily about making a sound. Just do it for a little while. Later see if you can pant three times without relaxing and taking a breath. You often feel this movement when sobbing or laughing. Add a little sound when ready.

Resonance

The more resonant your voice, the less effort you will need, the less likely you'll be to injure it, the richer it will sound, and the more powerful it will be.

- Still on the floor, give your face a good massage. Blow through loose lips. Move your head from side to side before bringing it back to the centre.

- Breathe in for four, hold for four, breathe out on a 'mmmmm'. Make sure the hum comes from your mouth as well as your nose (x4).

- Do the same again, start on 'mmmmm' and then open your mouth for 'AAAAH'. Feel how the resonance helps the richness and projection of the vowel sound (x4).

- Sit up slowly! (If you're too fast, you might feel dizzy.) Keep the back straight if you can. Circle the shoulders to relax them, and then do the last exercise again. Feel your lips with your fingers. Direct the hum to your fingers. Move your hand to the top of your head. Now make the sound, directing the vibration there. Now feel your chest. Direct the vibration to your chest.

Diction

Practising diction helps make your words clearer, and makes your ideas and characters more understandable for the audience.

- Chew vigorously. Make your face as big as you can/as small as you can.

- Stretch your tongue to your nose/then to your chin (x3).

- Tongue to the left/to the right (x3).

- Put the tip of the tongue on the outside of the teeth and roll it round the mouth each way (x4).

- Repeat putting the tongue on the inside of the teeth and circling the tongue (x4).

- Blow out through the mouth with loose lips.

- '*Tttt*' – '*llll*' – '*dddd*'. These are all tip of the tongue exercises.. Do each one three or four times, e.g. '*tttt tttt tttt tah*' (x4), Then '*llll llll llll lah*' (x4). etc.

- Then '*tttt llll dddd*' (x6).

- Do '*bbbb kkkk*'. Notice how with '*buh*' the sound is focused at the front of the mouth. '*Kuh*' is at the back of the mouth. Try '*pppp*' and '*gggg*' similarly.

- Finally, knit your fingers into a cradle, breathe in, and, turning the palms outwards, stretch to the ceiling. Breathe out and bring the hands back to the chest (x4).

- Now shake out the whole body for about twenty seconds.

- Check in with your body and experience how much more alive it feels.

Index of Exercises and Extracts

Page numbers refer to the page where each exercise first appears and is fully explained.

www.nickhernbooks.co.uk

 facebook.com/nickhernbooks

twitter.com/nickhernbooks